D0586122

NT

WITHDRAWN

Lincoln College

1094801

PLAY TO WIN
SNOOKER

PLAY TO WIN

SNOOKER

JIM MEADOWCROFT

WITH JOHN HENNESSEY

Nottinghamshire County Council

794.735

85013999

Leisure Services/Libraries

OCTOPUS BOOKS

First published in 1988 by
Octopus Books Limited
Michelin House
81 Fulham Road
London SW3 6RB

© Octopus Books Limited, 1988
All rights reserved
ISBN 0-7064-3158-8

Design by Laurence Bradbury Design Associates
Assisted by Sarah Collins

Line illustrations by Klim Forster
Diagrams by Oxford Illustrators Limited
All photographs were taken by Eric Whitehead except for
those on pp. 6, 69, 71 and 75, which were supplied by
Terry Smith, and the cover.

Project editor: Tessa Rose
Assistant art editor: Brazzle Atkins
Production: Audrey Johnston

Typeset by SX Composing, Rayleigh, Essex
Colour origination by Mandarin, Hong Kong
Printed in Hong Kong

Acknowledgements
The authors wish to thank the management of the Riley
Snooker Club in Reading for their kind cooperation. Thanks
also to Rothmans for allowing us the use of their facilities
during the Grand Prix tournament at Reading.

CONTENTS

Snooker's immense popularity grows by the season and stems from the fact that it is a game tailor-made for television; the table itself is the perfect shape for the television screen. An alert BBC producer realized back in 1969 that the game's colourful countenance offered the perfect vehicle to demonstrate the full benefits of colour TV, which had recently been introduced to this country. Thus, *Pot Black* was born. The one-frame series, spread over several weeks each year, became so popular that the millions who tuned in for a weekly diet of Ray Reardon, Eddie Charlton, Alex Higgins, John Spencer and Fred Davis, were quite happy to regard the competition as the world championship, a low-key event in those days. Then along came sponsors Embassy to revive an almost defunct world event and in so doing mirror the relentless pressure of life in Sheffield's aptly named Crucible Theatre. Suddenly billiard halls, once regarded with suspicion by right-thinking persons, were in vogue. Snooker centres complete with restaurants, bars and luxury surroundings soon replaced the threadbare, down-at-heel halls. It became fashionable to spend an evening at these clubs, and for much less than the cost of a night out at the local pub.

Respectability was the name of the game and the spectacular rise to fame of a young Steve Davis, guided by entrepreneur Barry Hearn, plus the continuing adventures of Higgins the Rebel, made the game even more watchable and even more accessible. Today, youngsters still not old enough to enter licensed premises can learn to play at most main centres under strict guidance from a resident coach. The countless hours of televised snooker, together with the universal availability of video machines, make it easy for any child with a thirst for knowledge to study at leisure his or her favourite player for hints on how to improve.

Snooker is the easiest game in the world to play badly. Through the antics of Steve Davis, Jimmy White and co., who make the game look

Wired for sound? Jim Meadowcroft (left) and John Hennessey relax in the ITV commentary box during an interval. They have been friends for years on the snooker circuit.

AUDIENCE PARTICIPATION

'Snooker is the only game in the world where we tell spectators to sit down, shut up or we'll throw you out!' – WPBSA chairman Rex Williams, joking about the strict rules imposed on snooker audiences

so simple, millions have flocked to snooker centres the length and breadth of Britain only to discover that it's a lot harder than it appears on television to strike one ball against another and knock it into a pocket.

That's not to say there's not tremendous satisfaction and enjoyment to be gained from playing at any level, provided you understand the basics of what can be a complex game.

John Virgo, the new chairman of snooker's ruling body (WPBSA) and one of the world's most respected professionals, says: 'There are some people who will play for 50 years and never pot more than a few balls at a time.' And he's right. Yet the game needn't be like that. Coaching at an early stage and learning good habits will certainly give you a better understanding and awareness of snooker and enable you to perform to the best of your ability.

Finally, my thanks to John Hennessey for unscrambling my thoughts over several weeks and putting them in order. *Play to Win: Snooker* may never put you in line for a slice of the £3½ million prize money available on the pro circuit, but we hope that the knowledge you gain from it will at least help you have fun knocking 15 red balls and six colours around that rectangular green-baize table.

EQUIPMENT

CHOOSING A CUE

It is often said that a player looks upon his cue as being even dearer to him than his wife or girlfriend. While this adage probably applies only to those in the top bracket, there is a certain amount of truth in it. The cue should be regarded as an extension of the arm. It is the most important piece of equipment for a snooker player but, unlike buying a suit, it is not possible to buy one tailor-made to meet your every need. Unfortunately there is a great deal of trial and error attached to finding a cue. The task is even harder these days than it was, say, 25 years ago. . . but when you come across the right one you'll know immediately and, hopefully, it will last a lifetime.

Steve Davis has become the greatest exponent of the modern game using an old ash cue he was given at the age of 16 in his father's local working men's club at Plumstead in south-east London. John Spencer, another of the all-time greats, was never the same player after his cue was smashed almost beyond repair in a car accident. By contrast, Alex Higgins chops and changes each season in the hope that he can find a replica of the ash model he used to win his first world championship in 1972. But more of what the stars reach for later.

Ash or maple?

Billiard halls abounded long before the advent of today's sophisticated snooker centres. In those days it was easy to go into a hall, select a cue from the rack, try it, discard it and move on to another simply because there was an extensive range of quality cues to choose from. The cue-making side of the business went into decline in the 1960s when good quality wood was suddenly no longer available. The old-timers had so much good timber to work with – like ash and maple for the shaft, and ebony (black or

marbled) or rosewood for the butt end. Davis's cue is a good example: it has an ash shaft and ebony butt. There aren't many cues around like that today.

Sadly, throughout the world there is a shortage of seasoned wood. Where a cue in the old days would be as straight as a die because the wood had been allowed to mature naturally, nowadays manufacturers don't have the time to go through the process of natural seasoning. As the game has taken off on a worldwide scale, so the demand for cues has been immense throughout Europe, Canada, Australia and, especially, in the Far and Middle East. What happens today is that the top cue-makers select the best quality wood available and use a kiln-drying process to stabilize the cue.

Obviously, if you are using a maple cue, say, in the humidity of Singapore, the wood would tend to sweat a little, become sticky and not run through the bridge hand as it should - but that's an extreme example.

Basically, there isn't much difference between ash and maple, but some players find themselves distracted by ash's heavy grain and prefer the close-grained maple. They want the smoothness, of course, but not the coarse grain staring at them every time they go down for a shot. Others won't even consider ash. Players from all walks of life, from the best professionals to the humble club players, have this problem with ash and so favour maple. But there's something about ash that gives it character. Alex Higgins always plumps for it. The point is to choose a cue that is fully compatible with you and your game; this is vital.

Getting started

What I have just discussed may seem far removed from the game of snooker itself, but I believe it is important to have at least a working knowledge of the tools and imperative to treat the cue with the utmost respect. Steve Davis attaches great importance to his cue and will entrust it to very few people. If he's giving a press interview after a match, his father Bill or driver Robbo can always be seen in the background minding the precious instrument. However, even Davis had to start somewhere, so let's assume you have never played snooker be-

REVIVAL MEETING

'Losing my cue was like losing my right arm, but fortunately a London company was able to make an exact replica and I'm playing well again.' – *Eddie Charlton on his return to form after a few years in the wilderness*

Total concentration as Tony Knowles lines up a shot with the rest secured firmly on the table. Note the inverted elbow of the cueing arm.

CHOOSING A CUE

fore but have been attracted to the game by a television match. There are two vital requirements to get you started: a cue and somewhere to play.

There is no benefit to be derived from walking into a sports shop and merely asking for a cue. You could end up out of pocket having bought something totally unsuitable. The answer is to call a local snooker specialist and seek advice from him. Most club managers are extremely helpful and will also offer good advice. There are usually a few decent players at every club, one of whom will no doubt help you get started and even offer guidance as to cue selection. As I stressed earlier, it really is trial and error which cue you choose to launch you in your new hobby. Unless you are a budding Jimmy White, it is doubtful whether you will be able to make accurate contact between cue ball and object ball immediately; that comes with timing, practice and good advice. What you should do from the 'off' is experiment with cues of differing weights, thicknesses and lengths.

Whether you are short, tall, heavy, slim or whatever has no bearing on the type of cue that will suit you best. A tall man might feel at ease with a small cue while a little fellow might adapt to a long one. Whatever you decide upon, do make sure the cue is absolutely straight. After all, you could hardly be expected to play with any accuracy with something resembling Robin Hood's bow!

The standard cue length used to be 4 ft 10 inches, but this was recently reduced by an inch. Curiously, the Australians use 5 ft cues. I know this to my cost because I was once involved in a deal shipping out 1,000 Hustler cue cases Down-Under for the Leeds professional John Dunning to his boss in Sydney. Lovely business, except that when they arrived the cues were too long for the cases!

A coach can help you with your stance, positional play and cueing, but the one thing he can't do is tell you exactly what cue you need. However, there are certain guidelines. I mentioned earlier the quality cue-makers and it is essential to look first and foremost for a brand name. If you can get hold of an old cue made by a reputable company that suits you, then guard it zealously. If not, settle only for the highest-

quality you can afford, like a Barracuda, and treat it with just as much respect.

If you do take to the game, you may want to consider having a custom-built cue from a private operator, like Hunt and O'Byrne in London, or John Parris in Kent. But be absolutely sure of your full requirements – balance, weight, etc. Who knows, in 50 years your cue may be as rare as the one Davis has today. You may be tempted to select a fancy one that costs a lot less than, say, a Riley cue. Resist that temptation, especially if the cue you have in mind is made in Hong Kong or Taiwan. You will soon discover its shortcomings and are better advised to play with cues supplied by your own snooker centre until such time as you can afford to buy a decent one.

The worst thing any player can do is to chop and change his cue from the outset, as I know from my own experience. It may be that you have damaged your cue and feel that the repairs are unsatisfactory. My opinion on what should be done in these circumstances has changed in recent years. Years ago there was an abundance of cues to move on to if you had problems. You had the comfort of knowing they were all good quality because they were tried and tested. People have now wised up and, as a consequence, there is a dearth of these collectors' items. I would now try everything to repair an old cue and, in fact, I have gained a reputation as a 'cue doctor' on the pro circuit over the years.

Two-piece or not two-piece. . .

All cues are roughly the same shape, but there are one-piece and two-piece models that come in various sizes. Let us now discuss the advantages and disadvantages of each. Once upon a time two-piece cues were regarded as a gimmick, but they have become standard equipment as more and more professionals favour them. While John Spencer was left cursing his luck at breaking his favourite cue, manufacturers were soon rubbing their hands together gleefully because he switched to a two-piece version in 1977 and promptly won his third world championship. That win paved the way for the two-piece cue to be accepted on a national scale, at a time when the snooker boom

SMOOTH TRANSITION

'My cue was shortened when I had to have the tip and ferrule replaced, so I had it converted to a two-piece. It hasn't affected my game in the slightest.' – *Steve Davis*

was just gathering pace, fuelled by extended television coverage. John's victory demonstrated that the two-piece could match the one-piece variety for accuracy, which had been the argument against its adoption.

The two-piece is certainly more convenient – as you will no doubt discover if you have to struggle on to a bus with a one-piece – and fits snugly into a small carrying case as opposed to one of nearly 5 ft. Higgins was once stopped at London's Heathrow airport after winning the 1981 Benson and Hedges final at Wembley with a one-piece cue and asked whether he had a rifle in his case! He was also a victim of John Virgo's cabaret act joke about the Irishman who bought a two-piece cue but couldn't find the instructions on how to piece it together. In fact, the two sections simply screw together.

Such is the quality of the two-piece cue today that it would be difficult even for the most experienced player to differentiate between the models and decide which one plays better. It is a question of what you are used to. Recently, Steve Davis, having broken the tip end of his cue, had a 30-hour 'operation' performed on it by John Parris to convert it into a two-piece model. 'I was a bit nervous when I first sawed it in half, especially as Steve was watching. Once I got started it was a fascinating exercise. Steve promptly won the Tennents UK Championship with his new, heavier, two-piece cue', said a delighted Parris.

Weight

Cues vary in weight from 16 to 20 oz. The standard weight is about 16½–17½ oz. Eugene Hughes wields an amazing 22-ouncer, the theory being that the heavier the cue the less work is required. Jimmy White has a heavyish 18-oz model, which shows in his spectacular power play, although such is his all-round game

that he has the deft touch of a player who uses a lighter cue. Stephen Hendry, the young Scot who has made such a big impression while still in his teens, uses a 17 oz; Terry Griffiths, another great performer, swears by an old cue which would be considered far too thin and too light for most players.

As with the ash vs. maple question, which weight of cue you choose is purely a matter of personal preference, again reached through trial and error. The key to finding the perfect cue is balance, then developing the timing to use it to best advantage. A player with a light cue is probably characterized by a long, flowing action and better touch than the player with a heavier one, which demands a different cueing action – more solid and staccato.

The tip

The tip is that little blue or green item on the end of a cue which requires chalk to help it 'bite' on the cue ball and prevent it from slipping, or miscueing.

Tips range from 9 to 11 mm in diameter. In theory, the bigger the surface the easier it should be to control the ball, but it isn't quite as straightforward as that for a complex game like snooker. Yes, you can strike the ball more easily with an 11 mm tip, but that size won't give you the reaction required for the finer points of break-building. The 9 mm tip demands more precision and consistency.

I would advise a newcomer to use at least a 10 mm tip and perhaps graduate to the smaller version as he or she gains experience. It was common practice in the old days for a player to start with an 11 mm tip and gradually, through a combination of wear and tear and sandpapering the end, finish up with a 9 mm tip!

You must learn how to maintain the cue. Sandpaper, once thought perfect for reshaping new tips, is outlawed. Each time sandpaper is applied, no matter how fine a grade it may be, a minute fraction of wood is shaved off which will in time affect the cue. It is not so much the balance that is affected, but the overall feel. The tip end is all-important and you must try to keep that as near to its original state as possible. When the cue needs retipping give it to an expert. It should be turned upside down and the

CUE TIPS/MAINTENANCE/TABLES

SMALL TIP

'John Spencer's tip is so small my wife could sew shirt buttons on with it.' – *Cliff Thorburn, after borrowing Spencer's cue in an emergency and losing 5-0*

brass ferrule used as a guideline for trimming the tip with a Stanley knife.

Higgins is often to be seen wielding a small file on his tip. He is either breaking up the chalk for more adhesion or simply trimming the edge slightly, possibly because he has been striking the ball on the same side each time, which leads to the tip leaning over. But that is a problem for when you get to an advanced level of play and not something to worry over at this tender stage.

Most players these days have learned how to retip their cues. John Spencer was an exception and always relied on manufacturers for maintenance work. What he didn't discover for a long time was that the person responsible for retipping his cue wasn't absolutely certain what he was doing, but this didn't become apparent until John noticed that the cue was much shorter and thinner than when it started out!

Selecting a good tip is as important as it is difficult. The sad fact is that from a box of 50 tips, you will be lucky to salvage 30. The test itself is simple: hold the tip between your thumbnails and squeeze the edge to gauge how much give it has. If the tip opens up like a concertina, which they can do, the fibres have gone and there is no point putting it on the cue.

What you should look for is a firm tip that holds chalk. Some players are under the illusion that a softer tip will give better reaction – better screw-back on the ball – but, in fact, it works in reverse. When you buy your cue it will already have a tip and I'm afraid you'll have to apply the rule of thumb to see whether it is up to scratch.

Maintenance

Sometimes during exhibition matches the public gets the opportunity to meet and chat to professional players. Occasionally a fan will pick up a player's cue and invariably express surprise at the smoothness. Players don't like their cues being handled by outsiders but the 'glassy' finish is no great secret. Any stickiness which may occur can be cured at a stroke, by wiping the cue down with a damp cloth, then 'polishing' with a dry one. A product called 'Cue Easy', which is a micro-abrasive, does the job to perfection.

That apart, always keep your cue in a case when it's not in use, never lean it against a wall or the side of the table when playing because it might topple over and, whatever you do, don't be tempted to meddle with it to alter the weight, length or balance. Seek expert advice if you are unhappy with the way it is playing.

The other equipment

Unless you have money to burn, it is highly unlikely that you will consider purchasing a table for your own home, which means you are in the hands of your local snooker centre. But as I stressed earlier, the centres and their equipment are these days usually top quality. Such is the competition to attract regular customers that a club would hardly dare take a chance on sub-standard tables or accessories.

Tables

Billiard tables, to give them their correct title, measure approximately 12 ft × 6 ft and vary widely in design and playing conditions. Naturally, you will almost certainly have a 'favourite' table at your own club, but it is advisable to play on as many different tables as possible in order to get a feel for them so that you are able to adjust your game accordingly.

For instance, some tables have what are known as 'tight' pockets while others are regarded as 'generous'. In 1986 Tony Knowles and Alex Higgins both complained bitterly that the championship tables had pockets like buckets, which favoured the out-and-out potters but not the more skilful players who rely on tight cue ball control and safety to produce openings. They weren't taken too seriously until Steve Davis added his weight to the argument about pockets being 'undercut'.

The actual opening size is a standard 3½ inches across, but depending on how the rubber cushion is cut into the pockets, they can

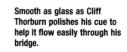

Smooth as glass as Cliff Thorburn polishes his cue to help it flow easily through his bridge.

EQUIPMENT

TABLES/BALLS/CHALK/RESTS

1. Ordinary rest
2. Spider
3. Half-butt
4. Grip-on cue extension
5. Swan-neck
6. Extended spider

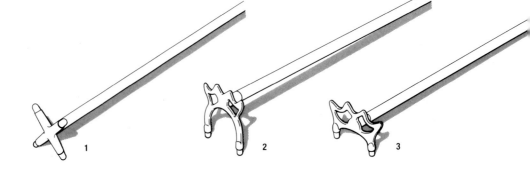

be generous or tight. The greater the undercut, the easier it is to pot balls, especially along the cushions.

Cushions can either have lots of bounce or be flat, which is easily discovered. Perhaps the most important factor is the green cloth, which contains a nap rather like the pile on a carpet. A worn cloth offers little chance of your being able to get much reaction from the balls, while a decent nap allows the chance of putting all the theory into practice. Hopefully, your club will take care to make sure its tables are level and will carry out regular maintenance.

Obviously, a table with big pockets would be beneficial to beginners, who could concentrate on learning straightforward potting and gradually work up to positional play. After all, how could you possibly maintain enthusiasm for the game if you couldn't carry out the fundamentals of knocking balls into pockets?

Many youngsters begin on a small home table and there are many tables on the market today which are good enough for the purpose of learning the rudiments of the game. Both Steve Davis and Stephen Hendry began their careers on a mini-table and graduated to the real thing once they had grasped the basic techniques.

Snooker Balls

There are 15 reds and six colours made of a synthetic substance called Super Crystalate and they measure 2⅛ in diameter. They are slightly lighter than the Crystalate balls used in the days of Joe Davis and co. and react much better to spin, which in turn allows players a much greater variety of stroke. Introduced in the early 1970s, some believe they are responsible for the many 'kicks' experienced by even the top players.

Chalk

That little blue or green cube players apply to the tip of the cue is essential because it increases the gripping power on the cue ball. That is why professionals are seen chalking the tip frequently and blowing away the dust. Higgins taps his cue on the rail to shed any surplus chalk dust which could lead to false contact with the cue ball.

Rests

Even 6-footers like Knowles and Davis can't reach every part of the table with their cues, and on occasions find use for a rest. There is always a variety to choose from, from the ordinary rest to be found sitting at either end of the table between small brackets, to the 'spider', which has a raised head to elevate the cue above another ball.

The ordinary rest (see illustration) is the most common implement used for shots that are just out of reach. You can see from its shape that it can be used in a low or a high position. Most club players tend to adopt the high position for every shot. The top players adopt the low position, which is more comfortable for plain-ball striking and for playing below centre for screw and stun. The high position should be adopted if you want to strike the white above centre to run the ball through.

The spider (see illustration) is raised much higher than the orthodox rest. It has three different cue positions and is shaped to allow you to cue over an intervening ball. This is a hazardous shot: the player is above the shot and has to strike downwards at an acute angle. Sighting is obviously difficult.

The half-butt (see illustration) is without doubt the most awkward of all the rests. It comes

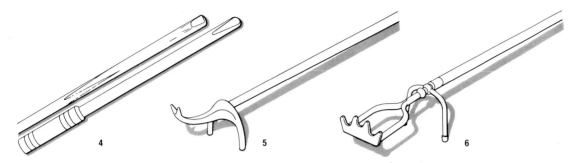

4　5　6

complete with an 8 ft cue which, in turn, has an outsize tip. Control is difficult, to say the least, because of the huge distance you are expected to cover with this unwieldy instrument.

These days most professionals and amateurs carry their own cue extensions (see illustration) and other pieces of equipment to minimize the risk of using anything but their own cue. Joe Johnson, Eugene Hughes and Tony Knowles use the Telecue, a conventional-looking cue which extends quite a distance at a twist. I'm not sure a top player would want to play with one full-time, but it is a marvellous innovation for long shots. Rex Williams introduced a gadget which attached to the rest to enable him to play awkward shots where the cue ball was tight to the cushion. Steve Davis has a similar mini-extension which allows him to cue over another ball with far greater ease than he would otherwise enjoy with the spider and which gives him a larger sighting area. For those length-of-the-table shots that everyone dreads, a threequarter butt is sometimes necessary. If you have to use either a threequarter or half-butt, avoid side and spin. Concentrate instead on making clean contact with the object ball.

Other rests to be found include the swan-neck and the extended spider (see illustration). Both are employed for extricating the white from those hard-to-reach situations, usually from among a cluster of reds.

What's up, doc?

It is always nice from my point of view when players approach me to ask: 'Jim, have you got time to have a look at the ferrule on my cue and can you retip it?' As we've said, players rarely let their cues out of sight and certainly wouldn't trust other players to mess about with them. But over the years I have gained a reputation for solving cue problems because I have always cared deeply about cues, and not just from the playing side.

The most dramatic repair I've undertaken came in the middle of the 1984 world championship when White was trailing 12-4 to Davis, having been involved in a thrilling semi-final against Kirk Stevens the previous night. Jimmy rushed into the commentary box at the end of the session and said 'Jim, I'm desperate for you to do something with the tip because it's as hard as iron.' The problem was he had no equipment with him and neither had I. 'I've got some Super-glue,' he added, so we took a calculated risk. I don't like using that product because if the tip doesn't go on exactly right it could cause all sorts of complications. Anyway, I retipped the cue then held my breath throughout the next afternoon as Jimmy came out with all guns blazing to win six in a row. With every frame he pulled back I kept thinking the tip was going to come off, but by the end of a memorable session he trailed 13-11. Unfortunately, he couldn't keep up the momentum but what a time to be asked to do a job. I'd never have forgiven myself had the tip fallen off, which did happen to him in another final a few years later. But I wasn't around that time.

Dennis Taylor, just days after winning the 1985 world championship, asked me to perform a similar task on his cue, although there wasn't quite the same sense of urgency. Other champions who have called on 'Doctor Jim' include Alex Higgins, in the early days, Willie Thorne and Cliff Thorburn. Twelve years ago I even fixed a new ferrule for Michael Ferriera, then world amateur billiards champion. It remains on his cue to this day – though not with the same tip!

THE BASICS
GETTING THEM RIGHT

Despite the boom in snooker's popularity, nothing generally has changed about the way the game is played. Conditions, perhaps, have altered, because the balls are lighter and the cloths often trimmed finer, but the basics still apply. Steve Davis picked up all his good habits from the Joe Davis books of snooker and even today he will consult his *Complete Snooker* volume when things go slightly off-key for him.

Few of the diagrams in this book are unique because the principles relevant in Joe's day are pertinent today. Remember, Joe practically invented snooker and all its shots (Higgins has introduced a few of his own since) and what he preached then still holds good. However, what I want to do is simplify the art of snooker. It is an extremely difficult game to grasp — technically perhaps the hardest of all games, billiards apart. Yet so many instruction books make such heavy weather of it that a youngster is more inclined to switch off than be eager to learn more about the game and how he or she can make real headway.

For starters, forget all about cue-ball control until you can pot with confidence. Don't worry about where the white lands up. You are not going to compile huge breaks after a few hours' practice, no matter how natural a talent you have for the game. Equally, it is impossible to master the art of side and screw and learn to pot at the same time. One follows the other naturally, but it does take time.

Once you have mastered the art of potting a red then a colour then perhaps another red, curiosity will almost certainly take over and you'll want to know how to play the white to carry on the break. It is possible to pot a number of balls through sheer good luck without really knowing how to control the cue ball, but there's no greater pleasure than playing, and getting perfect position for, your next shot. That can't be achieved unless you know how to strike the ball properly; how to wield the cue correctly; how to adopt the correct stance and how to address the ball in the proper manner. Many club players never manage to master any of the techniques,

1 2 3

A typical Alex Higgins pose: the ball struck, Alex is up like a shot to assess the result.

Far left: Fighting fit . . . as you can see, the boxer's stance is not dissimilar to that of a snooker player. The left arm (bridge hand) is ready to counter and the right (cueing arm) is poised to throw a punch (1). Holding that stance and keeping the feet perfectly still, drop the right arm to your cue on the table (2). Lean over from the waist, extend your left arm and bend the left knee (3). There you have the correct stance – give or take a degree or two for comfort. Note the feet; from start to finish of the sequence they have remained in the same position. Joe Davis advocated that the arm should be thrust straight out. Nowadays players tend to bend the left arm slightly with the elbow in place on the table. This stance gives the player a much more solid base and allows better cueing.

simply because they've never bothered to ask for advice. An hour or so with an experienced player or coach could make all the difference.

The true champion doesn't necessarily require a coach because snooker is very much a self-taught game, although in the early stages a good coach can often shorten the learning period. In some cases a good instructor can even enhance a champion's play by a slight adjustment. Steve Davis would turn to Blackpool coach Frank Callan whenever he felt his game was slightly off-colour and Frank was able to tell almost at a glance what was wrong. Terry Griffiths occasionally consults the same man for what could be termed a 'tune-up'. Many professionals, myself included, have had the benefit of

Frank's talent for spotting faults that may creep in unnoticed. Even the great players are seen to miss relatively easy shots on television, but that has more to do with pressure than lack of know-how and is an entirely different subject, which we will discuss later. For now, however, let's concentrate on the basics.

Stance

There's not much difference between the stance of a snooker player at the table and the pose adopted by a boxer; this analogy may sound a bit far-fetched but the feet are actually in a similar position as a player approaches a shot. Obviously the legs have to be still with the feet positioned at about five to two, if you can

17

THE BASICS

THE STANCE/THE GRIP

Whatever strength it takes to lift your cue off the table is correct for the grip you'll need to wield the instrument. Most beginners make the mistake of gripping the cue too tightly, making it impossible to cue freely and fluently. The correct grip is shown in 1 and 2, while 3 and 4 demonstrate how not to hold the cue. The butt must feel comfortable in the hand but be gripped firmly enough for you to control your shots.

1

2

imagine a clock face. The left hand is in defence and the right hand positioned almost as though you are about to throw a punch. You then drop down, or crouch like the boxer, bending from the waist upwards to the table and into the shot. There will be slight variations, depending on the height and build of the player, but it is an ideal guide to the correct stance for the beginner. Try it yourself and see how easily you slip from the boxing stance into that of the snooker player (see illustrations).

Throughout this book I will stress and stress again that all the theory and practice we discuss must not be allowed to detract from the natural talent a player may have, but there are important

SOUND ADVICE

'Snooker is a mind game. It is all about technique, and when a player loses form he has only one option – to go back to basics and discover what's going wrong.' – *Jack Karnehm, National Billiards and Snooker Coach*

basic rules which must be adhered to. Knowing where and how to stand, for example, gives your eyes a direct line to follow when making contact with the ball. That's not to say that if you don't stand with your feet in the exact position described above you won't be able to play the game. If you don't feel comfortable, minor adjustments must obviously be made.

Steve Davis will be my role model throughout because he plays the game to perfection and encourages only good habits. His stance, as you can see, is perfect. He tends to stand rather square. He gets down very flat for a tall man, almost as though his backside is above the level of his head when looking at him full on. This is a good position because the action of cueing is similar to firing a gun. A genuine marksman would never dream of firing from the hip like the Wild West gunslingers of old, and a top-class snooker player wouldn't contemplate taking a shot standing up. The reason is evident; you must see down the line of fire – down the barrel for a marksman and down the cue for a snooker player. It may seem daft to spell it out, but just take a look around your snooker centre and see how many players don't get down properly

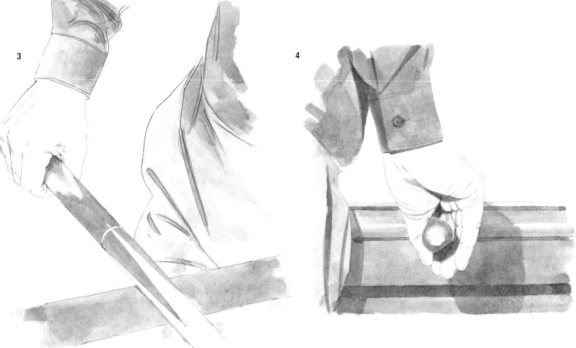

3

4

when they address the ball.Other leading players, such as Tony Knowles, adopt a similar pose to Davis. Alex Higgins is a law unto himself, but although he stands with his feet wide apart in a somewhat unorthodox fashion, the basic 'boxer's' rule is still evident.

Only recently a holiday-maker taking part in a Ray Reardon coaching week at a Pontins centre in Brean Sands, Devon, discovered he'd been standing incorrectly for 15 years. He'd made breaks of 90-plus in the past and was still capable of knocking in 40s and 50s with his league team each week, but after an hour's coaching he derived enormous benefit.

How to hold the cue

The grip and the stance are interrelated and together are as important to get right as any other aspect of the game. Most beginners tend to grip the cue too high at first, which restricts fluency as they address the ball and cue up to it. It is important that the cue isn't gripped too tightly and that you are comfortable with it from the start to give you freedom to develop your shots. A tight grip could lead to severe problems and, as you know, bad habits developed early in any sport

are difficult to rectify in later years. You could develop what we call a 'snatch' – stiffening the cueing arm and wrecking your timing.

The pressure it takes to hold a cue is no greater than that required to lift it off the bed of the table. I must emphasize the benefit derived from gripping the cue with the thumb and first two fingers – the index and third finger – only, which is where the control comes from, rather than holding it at the back of the hand. 'Gripping' the cue means holding the instrument in order to let it travel through the bridge hand (see illustrations).

Higgins grips the cue with his index finger pointing down. It looks rather clumsy and a little bit gimmicky, but perhaps his genius allows him to get away with it. Years ago it was his little finger that protruded. Why Alex has altered his grip I don't know, but obviously he feels it gives him a better touch. Who can argue with such a magnificent innovator?

Cueing up

In an ideal world we would all cue like Steve Davis, but that isn't realistic. Most world champions have perfect alignment – Ray Reardon is

THE BASICS

CUEING UP

Provided your stance is correct and you keep your body still on the shot, you should have perfect alignment. Look at the line from the point of the elbow to the tip of the cue. As you can see, it is straight. It is well worth enlisting the help of friends to check your alignment from both back and front.

If this sounds too fussy, wander around any snooker centre or billiard hall and watch the cueing techniques employed. It's a safe bet that the majority of people you'll see there won't be potting many balls, because perfect alignment is absolutely essential to good cueing.

the exception. He won the world title six times in the 1970s and is regarded as a snooker legend, yet he would be the first to agree that his cueing action leaves a lot to be desired. An accident in his younger days left him with a slightly deformed shoulder, which throws his elbow out of line as he cues.

The elbow should be vertical. If you look at a player full on, you should be able to draw a straight line from the tip of the cue over the bridge, through the centre of the chin (assuming he has 50-50 vision), the nose and the eyes, over the head and to the centre of the elbow (see illustrations).

The actual mechanics are very important. There should be no pronounced movement from the shoulder. All the movement is done from the elbow through to the wrist and the hand. The cue is moved in such a way that it forms the pendulum on a clock. Try tying a handkerchief to the butt and let the cue swing through the bridge freely.

One of the best natural exponents of cueing is Joe Johnson; that opinion might come as a surprise to one or two people, but he is a very fluent cueist. Despite the fact that Joe did practically nothing performance-wise in the 12 months after his surprise victory over Steve Davis in the final of the 1986 world championship, 1987 found him back in the final against the same opponent. He lost but in glorious fashion, giving Steve all sorts of problems in a match that provided a tremendous contrast of styles: a natural cueist against the man who is technically the best in the world.

It is absolutely essential that you keep still when striking the ball. I'm afraid it is one of my failings at times and even some top pros are guilty of moving in certain situations. Higgins is said to jerk his head on many shots, but a careful slow-motion study of him in action reveals that he is rock-solid until the point of impact when he tends to rise from the stance very quickly to get on with the game. Davis, on the other hand, stays down in line for ages, whether the ball is potted or not.

You must also make sure at delivery that you are cueing absolutely straight down the line and not cueing across the ball. This point relates directly to stance and grip. There's no way you

can line up the shot accurately if you are positioned incorrectly. A comparison with golf is appropriate here. Even if you feel comfortable when cueing up, ask one partner to stand behind you and another in front to check that you are properly aligned for the shot.

The actual art of cueing up is very much down to the individual. A player must feel comfortable on the shot and that he has enough time to play it well. It is important to discover the rhythm at which you play best and develop the habit of addressing the cue ball at a consistent pace. Terry Griffiths and Cliff Thorburn have been accused of slow play from time to time. Both players have a sound record of tournament wins. They play at the speed which is right for their game, and at which they feel comfortable, so you can't blame them for setting their own pace.

An awkward situation but
Steve Davis handles it
comfortably with solid
bridging into the pack.

Bridging

The basic bridge is quite easy to adopt. Simply place your left hand (vice versa if you are left-handed) on the table and spread the fingers a comfortable distance apart. The thumb is then pulled in to the index finger. Now press your fingers tightly into the cloth and try to draw them in towards the palm of the hand. This action will, of course, raise the fingers and so form the basic bridge required (see illustrations 1-4 overleaf).

The bridge hand is lowered or raised according to the shots needed. If you want to strike the top of the cue ball with the tip of the cue, the bridge should be at its highest level. A screwback shot demands that the ball is struck very low so the bridge would then be at its very lowest. Thus, the bridge itself determines where the tip will strike the white ball.

THE BASICS
BRIDGES

There are many different bridging techniques, but the easiest and most orthodox method is adopted by placing your left hand flat on the table (1), spreading the fingers comfortably apart, pulling the thumb into the index finger (2) and pressing the fingers tightly into the cloth. The action of drawing the cloth into the palm of the hand (3) automatically brings the fingers up to form the basic bridge. This bridge will suffice for most of your snooker, certainly in the early stages. You can see from 4 how easily the cue sits in the V-shape formed by the thumb and index finger.

The basic bridge is fine for open play, but there are occasions when the cue ball has to be played from awkward angles. The bouclé or loop bridge is ideal for playing the ball along the side of the cushion (5). 6 shows how the hand should be placed for those difficult-to-hit balls tight on the cushion which allow only a limited target area. The great safety players adeptly leave the cue ball as near to the baulk cushion as possible to lessen their opponent's chance of replying with a similar shot.

An easier variation of this bridge is seen in 7, which allows complete control without discomfort.

Bridging over an intervening ball is one of the most difficult shots to play (8), as it is so easy to nudge the ball slightly with your cue as you push it through. The most difficult bridge of all, it is worth practising this one regularly to reduce your chances of committing a foul stroke.

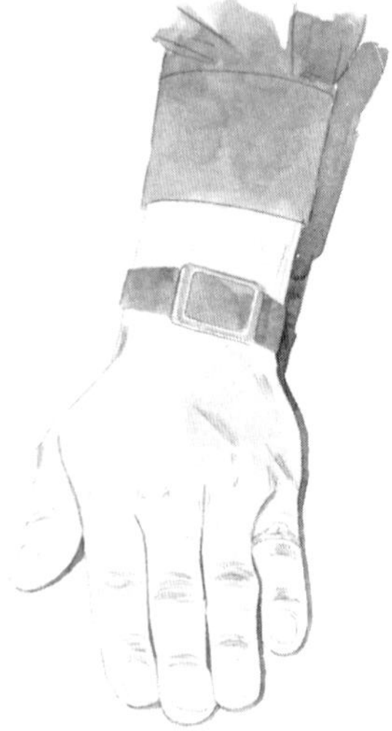

1

2

5

6

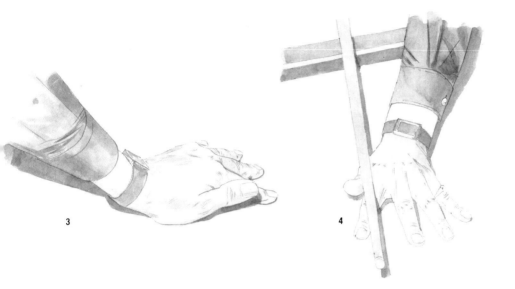

3

4

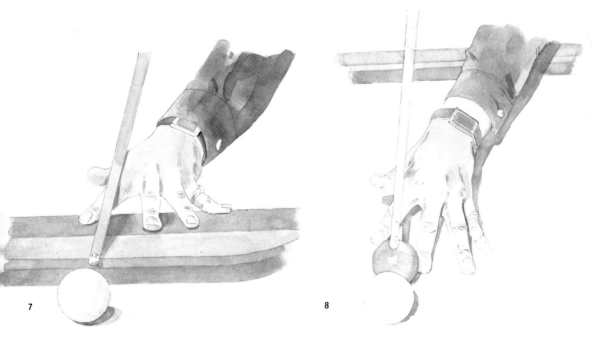

7

8

BRIDGES/USING A REST

9 shows the position of the bridge hand when playing the white out of the pack of reds. Again, this situation can be a minefield with a very real danger of your flicking another ball with the cue tip before or even after the stroke.

There are times when you'll need to adapt your bridge still further (10), perhaps to play other than a plain-ball shot. Experience will eventually guide you into the correct position for these.

9

10

Again, the bridge is very much a matter of personal preference. The usual position, as I said, is hand well spread with fingers about an inch apart, but there are variations. Terry Griffiths tends to use the forked bridge, with the index and other fingers quite well spread, as does John Spencer. Whichever style you opt for, the bridge you form must be sound. In other words, you must be confident that the bridge is solid enough for the cue to travel along it, and at the same time feel comfortable as you play your shots.

There are many times when you'll find you won't be able to use your normal bridge because of the position of the cue ball. Your hand and fingers will then have to adapt accordingly to the situation. The bouclé, a loop bridge, is used quite often by Higgins and Cliff Thorburn. It is employed either when a player can't

quite get his hand down the side of a cushion or he is concerned that the cue is going to fly off the bridge hand. The loop enables you to play such a shot without fear of mistake or miscue. There are no set names for the other types of bridge necessary for you to feel comfortable on a particular shot. The more awkward-looking positions are worth practising so that they become natural for when you need to adopt them in match-play (see illustrations).

Using a rest

The position of the body is reversed when using the rest. Whereas for an ordinary shot the player will stand side-on with his left foot forward, for rest play the right foot is forward and the cue is pushed through from the hand using only the lower arm, from elbow to wrist, for power. The elbow should be kept up, parallel to the table. When cueing normally the left shoulder is more prominent, but the reverse is true when using the rest; then, the right shoulder is foremost, as you can see from the photograph opposite.

The basic principles of cueing with a rest are: grip the butt firmly, and make sure your body is not behind the cue but rather at the side. Your elbow will invariably be resting on the table, which should give you some idea of the stance needed.

NATURAL ADVANTAGE

'I'm double-jointed, which makes it easy for me to form a bridge even in the most awkward situations.' – *Steve Davis*

USING A REST

Rest easy! Terry Griffiths shows how the ordinary rest should be used, with the arm holding the implement anchored firmly on the cushion.

OPENING SHOTS
LEARNING TO POT

Having selected a cue, sorted out the stance, the bridge and the alignment, now comes the moment when all the theories have to be put into practice and we strike the cue ball. It is not enough to jab the cue against the white ball, although that approach is common practice among club players. In order to generate the power required to screw the ball back or send it forward the tip of the cue must finish beyond the lie of the white, after the object ball has been potted.

There is only one shot that doesn't require the cue to travel through and that is the stun. With this shot the cue ball is held almost in position at the point it strikes the object ball while sending the red or colour forward. When you are playing that type of shot – making the cue ball stop dead on contact with the object ball – the cue is held back. It is still very controlled, however, and not jabbed or snatched. (Snatching is the tendency to tighten your grip on the cue involuntarily as the stroke is delivered, thus moving the cue, however slightly, from its intended line of aim.)

Club players experience most problems with the screw and stun shots because they don't fully understand what is happening. Instead of lowering or raising their bridge hand effectively to keep the cue parallel with the table, they tend to lift their elbow to form an angle with the cue. These problems shouldn't worry the beginner, however, who need only aim to pot the ball with confidence at this stage.

Cueing test
The following exercise will test your cueing. The aim is to strike the cue ball dead centre and play it the length of the table (see diagram. far right). Place the cue ball on the brown spot and put a little chalk mark directly behind the black spot. The cushion beyond is the point of aim but it is difficult to see the black spot when you are on line and down on the shot, hence the chalk mark. If the ball returns in a straight line, it means you've struck it well. Try to keep the cue level, with the tip and butt exactly in line. Stay down on the shot and keep absolutely still, leaving the cue where it finishes after you play the shot. Stand up and check the amount of follow-through you've used (see line illustration).

Naturally, the shot would have to be played at soft, medium and hard strength to test your cueing even further. The harder you hit the ball, the more difficult it is to keep it in a straight line. Power is essential in snooker today, as Jimmy White demonstrates, but it also means you have to be extremely accurate when hitting the ball with full force.

Potting
The first step towards playing snooker now taken, the next is to strike the white against another ball, known as the object ball, and pot it. This skill either comes very naturally from the beginning or takes much longer, depending on the player's ability to grasp the rudiments. Absolute beginners can find this stage of the game extremely frustrating. You may have to crawl a little before you can even contemplate walking, especially if you want to do well and have set yourself a tough target.

Potting balls is not something that can be taught easily, and it helps if you have natural ability or a feel for the game. A knowledge of angles cannot be had immediately by the novice, but sheer perseverance and a willingness to learn through trial and error should pay off eventually. The knowledge gained can then be stored in the memory bank forever.

It is no coincidence that the top players rarely miss a black off the spot. They will have played all the angles a million times in practice or during a match.

As you progress you will find it necessary to develop a fluent cue action, one that gives the eye, hand and, most important, the brain, time to co-ordinate the strokes. To do this, try and develop a pause at the back of the final approach to your shot, which allows the eye to look clearly through the line of aim. Then, as though you are sighting a rifle, 'fire' the cue through the shot. This timing will help reduce the snatch and jab referred to previously and thus improve your accuracy.

Later, you will learn to paint a mental picture of how to play the shot and of how the ball will react when struck.

Sometimes, of course, what seems to be a simple miss is a lot tougher than it appears from my position in the commentary box. The spec-

STRAIGHT MAN

'I don't have time to laugh and joke during a match, because snooker is an extremely hard game to play and requires total concentration.' – *Steve Davis on why he's got a poker-face image*

tators' 'oohs' and 'aahs' don't usually indicate much other than their interest in the match because they have no way of knowing what type of shot the player was attempting. There might only be a few inches between white and object ball, and the pot itself might seem to present no problems. The art of the game, though, lies in placing the cue ball in the correct position for the next red or colour, and in order to do that the player may have to use complex spins. So, next time Higgins or White misses what looks like an easy shot you'd get nine times out of ten, spare a thought for him.

Snooker is a fascinating game, almost like chess except that it's physical. A chess player has to work out in his mind where to make the next move, but the actual doing is not difficult. He can even pause halfway through the action and have a rethink. In snooker, however, working out a shot then carrying it off can be equally difficult because a player will tend to tense up, so preventing the cue from travelling quite as easily and consistently as it should. For this reason you must try to do everything correctly from the beginning and not just hit the ball around aimlessly. Strict practice routines should be carried out to test consistency day by day, otherwise when your form deserts you it will be difficult for you to assess what is going wrong with your game.

One of our primary aims in this book is to start you off on a sound footing by giving you a thorough understanding of the basics. If you get these basics right, you'll find it much easier to identify your faults later on, should the need arise.

Potting straight

Let's start with a simple shot: potting the blue off its spot into the middle pocket from a distance

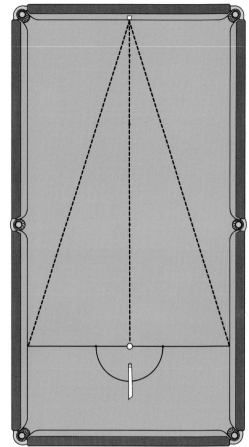

Left: Learning to cue correctly, straight and using side. Place the cue ball on the brown spot and aim for a chalk mark on the top cushion immediately behind the black spot. If you have made proper contact with the cue ball, it should pass over the blue, pink and black spots and return to the brown spot. Using side is one of the hardest parts of the game, as you will discover in the next chapter. For now we need identify only the basic principles of side and how it differs from plain ball. The following simple exercise should help. From the brown spot again, aim to hit the chalk mark but this time strike the ball on the left side. Repeat the shot but striking the ball on the right side. Note the effect that each shot produces. You can vary the angle of shot by experimenting and trying different degrees of side and weight.

Below: Gauging the amount of follow-through on a shot: top, cueing up from the brown spot; bottom, after the cue ball has been firmly struck. Note where the cue tip has finished.

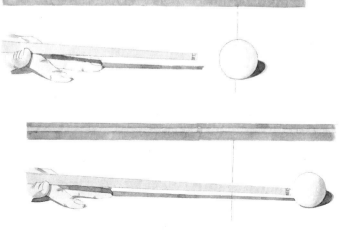

OPENING SHOTS

Perfect control from Alex Higgins. There is no movement as the 'People's Champion' lines up this shot.

of 8 inches or so (see diagram). This is the most straightforward shot in the book as there are no angles on the pocket to contend with. It is the logical first shot too because it will expose any basic flaws in your technique.

Take your time and strike the white ball gently but firmly in the centre with a straight cue, using all the hints we have discussed so far. The white ball should roll forward a few inches. Repeat the shot a few times until it feels comfortable, then increase the distance between the balls by a few inches. This practice will give you an idea of what the game is all about – and also that lovely feeling of seeing the ball disappear down the pocket. It is a strict discipline and an essential one if you are going to learn about potting balls.

Potting on a diagonal

Once you have mastered the first, simple exercise, try potting the ball on a diagonal line between corner pockets (see diagram). Place the cue ball on the baulk line where the diagonal crosses, with the object ball a foot or so away in the same line. It's another straight pot and on paper at least it looks as easy as the centre pocket pot. However, you will soon discover that the angle of the pocket has altered, which will make life a little more difficult. The greater the distance between balls, the greater the risk of inaccuracy, so it is imperative to practise and practise. John Spencer calls it 'grooving the action' – a description for it that's as good as any.

LEARNING TO POT

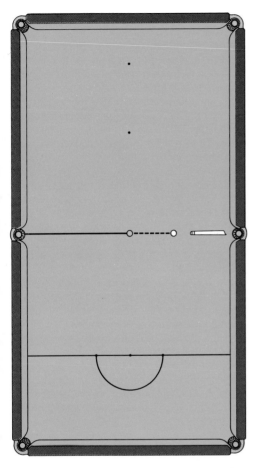

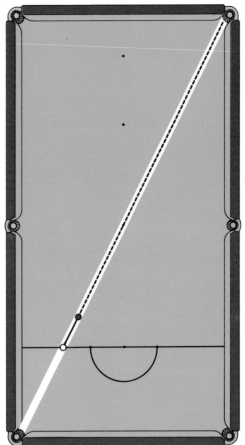

Far left: Potting blue off its spot is an easy exercise for the novice and is intended to help cueing technique. Once this exercise becomes easy, experiment by gradually increasing the distance between the two balls.

Left: This novice exercise is invaluable because it is the first attempt at potting at an angle. The target area (the pocket) isn't as generous as it is full on. (See text, 'Potting on a diagonal')

I realize that this exercise could become very tedious for a beginner. One way to enliven interest after a long practice session is by scattering a few red balls around the table with the colours and try potting them. You will no doubt be alarmed to discover how vast the table appears at first and how difficult it is to control the cue ball enough to string shots together.

Learning the angles
Once you have mastered the technique of straight potting, you can then start thinking about angled potting, using the same learning procedure with the cue ball. You can discover the effects of coming around the angles of the table by using plain ball methods, as demonstrated in the diagrams. There are key shots that crop up from time to time and if a player has the know-how to carry them out successfully, he can create openings from which to win a frame.

The only way to find a true potting angle is by experimenting. An excellent routine for developing angled pots can be devised around the black spot. Leaving the black on its spot, place

---

THE SECRET OF SUCCESS

'The game's not all about century breaks. It's the forties and fifties that win frames.' – *Steve Davis*

OPENING SHOTS
LEARNING TO POT

Potting black off its spot from various angles is a good exercise to practise regularly. Do not, however, concentrate on the recognized angles alone and thus forget those in-between angles.

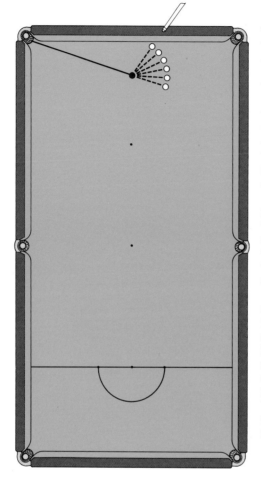

the cue ball some 2 feet away from the black, then from a quarter-circle area, and at various angles, pot into either of the top pockets. In practice there are only a few angles to concern yourself with, ranging from full ball (face on) with no angle to a fine cut. Between these extremes there are three distinct angles: threequarter-ball, half-ball and quarter-ball, which are self-explanatory. There are countless variations between these distinct angles, but knowledge of how and when to use them will only come with experience.

Only practice can enhance these particular potting skills and enable you to recognize which type of shot is required in a given situation. If you miss consistently from one angle, you will obviously need to make an adjustment until you hit the right one, but do check your cueing action and timing first.

The black ball routine is a critical one to master. Its purpose is twofold. First and foremost it teaches the dominant shot in professional snooker, from its many angles. Secondly, it equips players for major break-building and should be used for that purpose whenever possible. For a majority of club players, building a break seems to represent a big stumbling block. The black ball routine could help break down a few psychological barriers as well as teach you the angles.

No one seems to have the answer to this problem – or perhaps they are too bemused by the unusual technique of Terry's opponent (opposite).

THE MYSTERIES OF SPIN
STUN AND SCREW SHOTS

There are various degrees of spin which can be applied to the cue ball by using 'side', 'screw', 'drag', 'swerve' and 'masse' shots to enhance your game. Plain-ball potting is fine but it does restrict positional play, especially when break-building. The various spin techniques achieve the effect of altering the normal course of the cue ball after it has made contact with the object ball.

The pack of reds sits there waiting to be shuffled to develop a break, around the black spot area preferably, but even the world's greatest potter couldn't possibly hope to achieve a worthwhile total without employing spin.

There are certain key shots that have to be played in order to make sizeable breaks because particular angles demand them. The two forms of spin most employed in the professional game for break-building are 'stun' and 'screw' (when the cue ball is struck below centre), as you'll probably have gathered from TV commentaries, which are littered with references to them.

Stun shot

As the name implies, this method halts the cue ball in its tracks after striking the object ball. Like screw, the basis of this shot is backspin. This shot allows you one of the few opportunities in a match of knowing exactly where the cue ball will come to rest, provided the shot is played properly. The closer the balls are together, the less stun you need (see diagram).

Screw shot

This shot enables the white to travel back towards you after impact with a red or colour. The bridge needs to be lowered to play screw. The easiest way is to roll the hand inwards, as if turning it on its side, while maintaining the firmness. The thumb will then drop automatically, thus lowering the channel for the cue to pass through.

The screw shot helps reduce the novice's natural fear of ripping the cloth with the top of his cue – that's been known to happen, but only because the player hasn't understood that to play a screw shot the cue must be kept parallel by dropping the bridge. Once it is accepted that the cue itself is not dipped by raising the elbow, even the rookie's tendency to jab at the ball should be minimized. To achieve the desired effect, you must follow through correctly.

Chalk is invaluable for 'stun' and 'screw' shots and enables the cue to 'bite' on the lower part of the white ball. Professionals will use these shots many times during the course of a match, which is why they chalk the tip of their cue constantly.

Exercise

The same set-up that we used for the basic exercise (see diagram, p.29) with the white and the blue ball on its spot is ideal for learning a simple screw shot. Line the white up about 8 inches away from the blue going across the

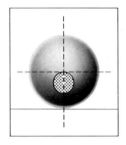

Above: A stun or stop shot is played below dead centre, which kills the cue ball's forward movement, stopping it instantly on contact with the object ball, provided the two balls are in direct line with a pocket.

Right: An easy way to demonstrate stun, leaving the white on the blue spot after potting the colour.

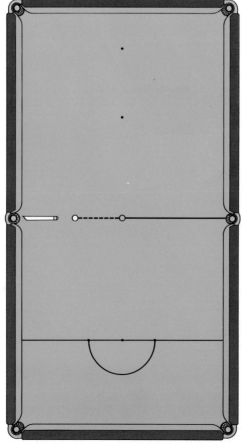

Almost a smile from Dennis Taylor as he attempts to hold the cue ball while sending the brown to the top of the table. At first glance this shot looks like a massé but Dennis is, in fact, digging as deep as possible into the white.

THE MYSTERIES OF SPIN

SCREW/SIDE/DRAG

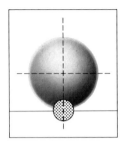

Above: A screw shot propels the ball forward then spins it back; you can create the effect yourself by bringing your hand down sharply on the back of a ball, in a chopping motion. For the shot itself the ball is played well below centre. The contact point varies with individual players and the amount of backspin required.

Right: Potting blue off its spot, using screw. The aim is to bring the white ball back into the pocket nearest you and pot the blue at the same time. Try increasing the gap between the two balls when you become proficient but, remember, the cue must follow through – and lower that bridge hand!

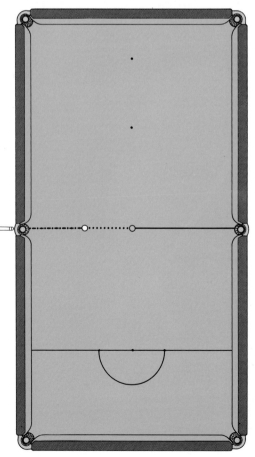

table and keep potting the ball using screw (see diagram).

By this stage of your fledgling snooker career you will be starting to leave the novice tag behind you. The game will appear much simpler as you discover more about screw techniques. Experimenting is, again, the key to understanding how the ball reacts to screw. You will find with practice that a simple screw shot is no more difficult than a simple plain pot, yet it opens up so many more exciting possibilities.

Experiment by striking the cue ball just below centre and thereafter in positions down the vertical line of the ball. As your confidence increases, you will begin to regulate the amount of backward rotation you achieve from each position until you are able to draw the white ball

back into the centre pocket while potting the blue at the same time.

To increase your learning, experiment with the firmness of your grip and the position of your hand on the butt of the cue. You will soon find more and more variations and higher degrees of accuracy will develop.

Stun run-through

A third possibility with spin is the stun run-through shot, which enables you to run the cue ball through a few inches but not as far as it would travel if you'd used a plain-ball shot. The cue ball is struck higher than for a normal stun shot but still below centre. By striking the white ball slightly more firmly, you are reducing the chance of its running off course.

Side spin

The use of side is the hardest part of the game to master and in your novice state it would be best almost to ignore it. However, do experiment. Strike the white ball straight up the table hitting it on the left or right-hand side – be careful not to cue across the ball but keep your cue in line, butt to tip. Watch and absorb how much the ball reacts right or left from the top cushion. (See diagram on p.35.)

As you gain in experience, experiment by striking an object ball using side and watching how it reacts as the white makes contact or strikes a cushion. Side played away from the desired path of the object ball is called running side, which widens the angle and speeds the ball from the cushion. Side played in the direction you want the object ball to take is called check side, which narrows the angle and slows the white ball.

Every cloth has a directional finish in the weave called the nap, which runs from the baulk end of the table to the top (see illustration). When a ball is played very slowly against the nap it will be seen to pull towards the baulk pockets. If side is applied, the ball will often run in the opposite direction as the weave of the cloth takes effect.

Drag

When you feel confident and competent enough to play the shots we've covered so far in

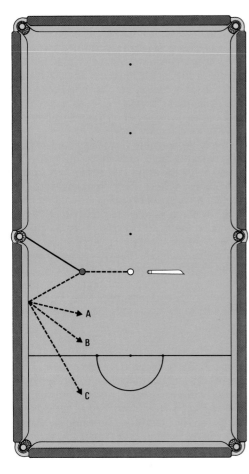

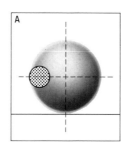

A

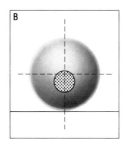

B

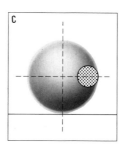

C

Far left: Two different applications of side which enable the cue ball to deviate from its usual angle off the cushion (B), or on contact with the object ball, to enhance positional play. For check side (A) the ball is struck on the same side as its intended direction of travel. This has the effect of narrowing the angle and contrasts with running side (C), which widens the angle off the cushion.

The nap on the green cloth is like velvet. Brush it one way, from baulk to black spot, and it is smooth; brush it the opposite way, and there is a rough feel. A ball travelling in the direction of the nap reacts differently to one being played against it, especially when spin is applied to the cue ball. Right-hand side on the white played from baulk takes the ball to the right and left-hand side to the left. From the opposite direction, however, right-hand side takes the ball to the left and vice-versa with left-hand side.

This is a technical subject and not one a beginner should be concerned with, but as players progress they have to take the nap into account to ensure accurate positional play.

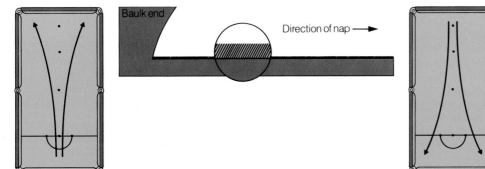

Baulk end

Direction of nap ⟶

THE MYSTERIES OF SPIN
DRAG/SWERVE/MASSE

Playing a shot using drag is very advanced play and demands the utmost skill. Drag is used to send the ball a long way up or down the table and leave it there. It is possible to run the ball, but at the risk of it being thrown off course by the table. Drag enables you to have full control over the ball. For this shot the ball is struck very low with normal cueing power, as though you were playing a screw shot. The effect will be to send the white up the table at considerable speed until the backspin slows the ball as it reaches its target. As you can see from the diagram, to hold the white for the black would be impossible were it not for drag.

Drag can also be used for safety. For example, it could allow you to send an object ball to baulk yet hold the cue ball at the top of the table.

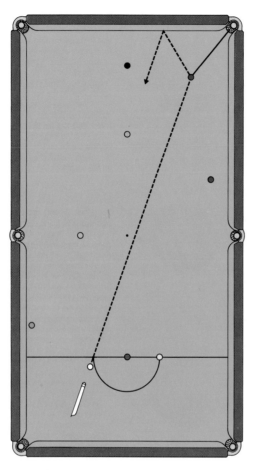

ers. Once a player has become proficient at playing the swerve shot, he can often get himself out of difficulty by manoeuvring the white around an intervening ball rather than using a couple of cushions to make contact with his target ball. The difficult part of the shot is that you're never quite certain what degree of contact you're going to get on the object ball, but have to trust in Lady Luck.

In this instance the player can't aim for the object ball but has to allow for the cue ball to get round the intervening ball *before* the swerve actually takes effect. Thus, he's aiming not only to miss the intervening ball but also the object ball. To get the desired effect the butt of the cue is lifted in the air, depending on the degree of swerve required, and the tip dug in towards the top of the white ball. The swerve will only take effect once the cue ball has successfully negotiated the barrier in front of it, and will then make an arch shape and come back to its original line. Needless to say, there should be no cue follow-through.

Massé

This is a billiards shot and not commonly used in snooker. It can be useful for creating an angle, though not in the normal alignment method. Massé may best be described as an extreme form of swerve, and is used in similar situations. The cue is inverted and an angle created to swerve the white around an intervening ball, sometimes to escape from a snooker or occasionally to pot a ball you wouldn't normally be able to get at without striking one or two cushions first. It is a difficult shot requiring great

this chapter, you can introduce the drag shot. Its purpose is to add a little more pace to your stroke to ensure true running while controlling more accurately the speed of your white ball when contact has been made. To play the stroke come below the centre of the white and strike the ball as if you intend it to stop in its tracks without hitting anything! Watch the ball as it runs and observe how its rotation appears to reverse as it travels up the table. The drag shot is ideal for control over distance but beware – if your cueing is poor, it will accentuate your faults.

Swerve

This shot is an extreme type of side and is used in the majority of cases to escape from snook-

DREAM SHOTS

'Alex can play shots the rest of us can only dream about.' – *Ray Reardon on Higgins' extraordinary ability*

The man himself could not have found fault with Ray's judicious assessment of his skills:

'I can play shots the other players can only dream about.' – *Alex Higgins on his extraordinary ability*

MASSE

Neal Foulds kneels to get an eye-level view of the situation – a useful ploy for determining whether or not a ball will 'go.'

skill of the player. It needs no follow-through, obviously, and has to be played with a lot of conviction. Even though it demands quite a bit of power, there's a delicate way to play it once mastered.

Summing up, Steve Davis plays snooker with the absolute minimum of allowance for side, while the boy who would be king, Stephen Hendry, plays all the flair shots with 100 per cent side, swinging the cue ball around the table as opposed to playing it more directly. It's not for effect that young Stephen plays this way but

because it is his natural style. After the brilliant season he's had in 1987-8, there will be many youngsters inspired to copy his flamboyant way of playing snooker.

Steve, on the other hand, has perfected the modern-day art of snooker by eliminating all the risk elements and playing the shots in a way consistent with his strict percentage game, reducing the chances of error. He is without doubt the purist, the players' player, although the general public would probably argue that Alex, Jimmy or Stephen are far more exciting to watch.

PRACTICE MAKES PERFECT

ROUTINES: TV LINE-UP

All snooker players should have the discipline to practise. There are many different ways of practising and, whichever method you choose, it should have a point to it and not be aimless. Beside the fun and pleasure to be had from the game, hard work is required if you are to get full satisfaction. There was a time when you could see young fellows, in particular, hitting balls around in billiard halls with no real thought or application. Now, televised snooker has not only given promising players a taste for the game but also a feel for how it should be played. They watch their heroes playing to perfection and want to emulate them.

If you have arrived at this chapter having worked your way through the book, the chances are you will be ready for practice routines. These will act as a guide to your form as much as to your ability and will provide an accurate yardstick by which you can measure your rate of progress.

TV line-up

As a youngster making my way through the amateur ranks with Dennis Taylor and Alex Higgins during the late 1960s and early 1970s, I used what was known as the 'TV line-up' to assess my progress. It was an exercise devised by the great Joe Davis and involved spreading all the reds in a straight line between blue and black balls, then potting red–colour, red–colour in sequence, as you would for a normal break. The idea was that Joe would eventually make a century break on television. He did manage a century – the film was discovered in the BBC archives only a few years ago – but in a match and not using the 'TV line-up'.

You can see from the diagrams how the theory works. To be successful, a player would have to use all the various potting skills I hope you will have grasped from earlier chapters.

An average player would at first hope to pot a couple of reds with blue, pink or black balls, perhaps, then progress in stages until he or she is able to clear enough red balls to compile a century. The next target is the magical 147 maximum, sinking 15 reds, 15 blacks and all six colours in sequence. I know what a thrill it was for me when I managed the feat after some two years of trying. From the start, though, I was

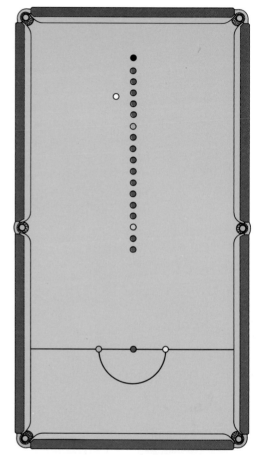

The TV line-up is the best of all practice routines for developing close control. It teaches perfect cue ball control and tells you more about the way you are cueing than any other exercise. The prime target is 100. The 15 reds are spread in various patterns in a straight line between the blue and black balls. A beginner might have five between black and pink, a further eight between pink and blue with the remaining two below the blue spot. The object is to build breaks in the conventional manner by potting red-colour, red-colour in sequence.

So, placing the cue ball at a convenient starting point, let's run through the various shots which are employed to get the momentum going. It is doubtful whether a beginner would pot more than a couple of reds with a couple of colours, but as he or she progresses so the tally will mount.

1 Nicely in position to pot the first ball, which is the second red in the sequence down from the black.

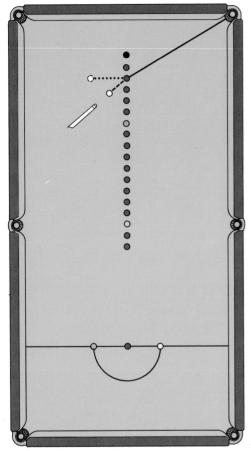

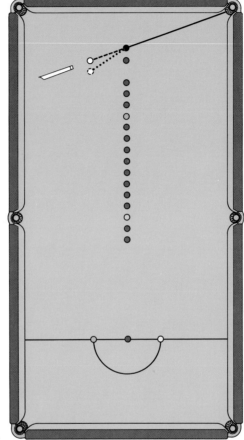

2 The red is on its way to the pocket and, thanks to a little stun shot, the white is travelling across in perfect position for the black.

3 A little screw shot sees the black safely down and the white placed nicely this time for the first red in the sequence. The black has disappeared but the white hasn't the desired angle.

PRACTICE MAKES PERFECT

ROUTINES: TV LINE-UP

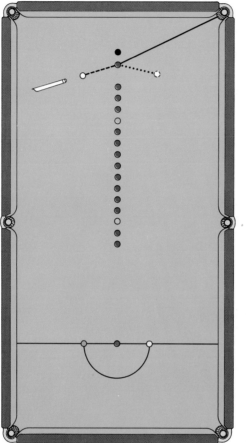

4 This time a stun run-through shot has to be executed on the red to take the cue ball to the other side of the line-up for the first time.

5 A screw-back off the nearside cushion is needed to keep the break going. Just look where the cue ball ends up, perfectly in line for a choice of reds.

ROUTINES: TV LINE-UP

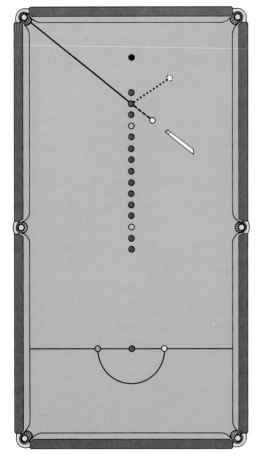

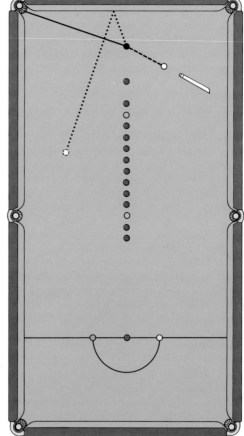

6 Another small screw-back with stun leaves the white ball on a good lie for the black.

7 The black is potted, thanks to top spin and right-hand side, which corrects the angle of the cue ball as it comes off the top cushion and brings it back into a prime position for a choice of reds to the corner or middle pockets.

As you can see, for this routine I have used quite a variety of shots and spin to keep the cue ball around the black spot. In a short space of time I have potted three reds and blacks and there is a choice of reds to maintain the break.

able to see how much my skills were improving whenever I attempted the exercise. These days, sadly, this particular form of practice is regarded as dated but, personally, I believe it is as good a test as any to check your game – and at least there is a fun element to it.

Twelves
There are many variations on the line-up. Frank Sandell, who has contributed a chapter on junior coaching later in the book, is a great believer in Twelves and is certain that particular exercise hasn't been outlined in any instruction book before. Highly-skilled players would probably scoff at Twelves but it is an excellent way of learning cue-ball control, weight of shot and the pace of the ball. As you can see from the diagram, 12 reds are lined up in pairs at right-angles to the centre of each pocket. The idea is to pot all 12 balls in the least number of shots. In order to achieve that goal, you must not dislodge the balls on the inside. It is really an excellent fun routine and should appeal to those just starting out.

Twenty-ones
Another form of the line-up is a straight all-in-a-line 21-ball, again an exercise which is designed to test your cueing and knowledge of angles. This is not only intended for beginners; the more experienced player can make it more fun by setting a number of shots in which to clear the table (see diagram far right). Later, when this exercise has also become easy, vary the practice by cutting out all shots against the cushion.

Another way of taking the tedium out of practice is to scatter all the balls around the table, but away from the cushions, and pot them in no particular sequence. Wherever you land there is sure to be a pottable ball. This routine, called 'easy twenty-ones', is invaluable for keeping your confidence high (see diagram).

How the stars practise
Even if the line-up doesn't appeal as a routine, promising players should be prepared to practise for at least a couple of hours every day. Consistency is the name of the game, as Steve Davis has demonstrated time after time. It isn't luck that he's won more titles than the rest of the

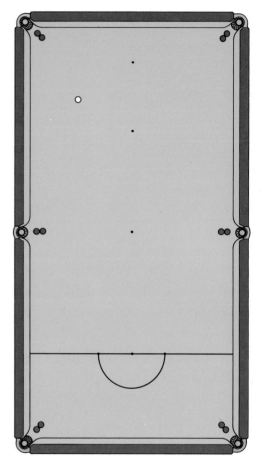

Twelves is an invaluable practice routine for beginners, and is more difficult than it looks. It teaches control and weight of shot. Using plain-ball only, pot all 12 balls in as few shots as possible, but not two at a time! The object at each pocket is to pot the first ball and leave the second for your next shot.

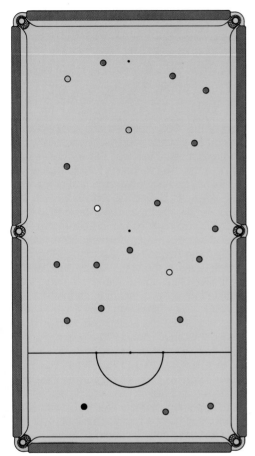

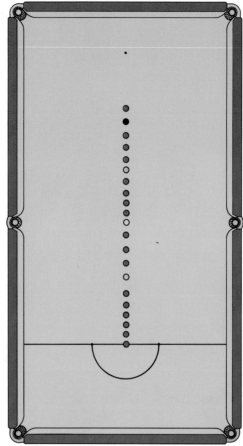

Easy twenty-ones provides ideal potting practice. Scatter all the balls around the table, keeping them away from the cushions, then pot them in any order. Concentrate on laying another ball 'on' from every pot you make. By so doing you will eventually have covered every angle on the table. You'll find that cue ball control becomes more vital the longer the practice continues and the number of balls on the table decreases. Make a note of your score each time you play this game, and aim to beat it.

Twenty-ones is excellent practice for learning the potting angles and cue ball control. Spread all 21 balls between brown and pink or black spots, then pot them in any order, counting the shots. Gradually, you should reduce the number of shots it takes. Once you can pot all 21 without missing, make the game tougher by not playing the white against the cushions – that's a real test of ability.

PRACTICE MAKES PERFECT
HOW THE STARS PRACTISE

Note the height of the cue butt, which is necessary if Steve is to see the shot. Davis's height (6 feet) gives him an advantage over most players.

BURNING AMBITION

'I want to be world champion and No. 1, and I'll practise and practise day and night until I make it.' – Jimmy White

start of the 1986-7 season and decided on a new method of attack on the championship he treasures most. (Such was Steve's determination to regain his title that he took to walking 10 miles a day to improve his stamina.) For years he had practised behind closed doors with his father as sole spectator. Davis decided to integrate his rigid routines with proper match-play against some of the top amateurs at his Matchroom club in the Essex market town of Romford.

Nick Lazarus, son of the former First Division footballer Mark and a gifted amateur, was recruited as a No. 1 'sparring partner' for the world No. 1, together with Tony Putnam, who once worked at the Matchroom and is rated among the top amateurs in the country, and a relative old-timer, Norman Buck.

Steve quickly realized that there could be more to practice than simply playing the same shots over and over in isolation. He demanded that his playing partners re-enact match-play situations rather than scatter the balls over the table and have potting contests.

Steve, one of only three players to have made TV maximums, knows better than anyone that the most telling breaks are those that win frames and that from the last red or two a break of 36 can be just as deadly as an early 60 in the same game. He reasons, correctly, that good break-building is important but that it's not vital to smash world records every time he steps up to the table. The results of Steve's new practice routine were quite startling. Young Nick Lazarus gained a new 'mate' and Davis learned the value of practising with others for company. 'Nick is a very gifted amateur, perhaps too talented for his own good because he doesn't always treat his opponents with enough respect,' said Steve, after recapturing the world title.

Lazarus, too, benefited. 'I didn't get much chance to play my shots, but I became a first-class fielder,' said young Nick. 'I spent most of

snooker world put together. From his early teens, he has applied himself diligently to the purpose of eliminating errors from his game. His goal has demanded up to five hours of solid practice daily for weeks on end, especially during preparation for the world championship. Interestingly, after losing his second successive world final at the Crucible Theatre in 1986, Steve decided to alter his monastic routine drastically. He took a long hard look at his game before the

the time picking balls out of pockets and respot-ting them for my mate Steve.' It's the sort of opportunity most youngsters would die for, but Nick took it all in his stride. Unfortunately, though, his own game never really reached the heights on the pro-ticket series of tournaments that season and he was left waiting in the wings to move out of the amateur ranks while one or two other less gifted players were rewarded for consistency. For Lazarus it was a painful lesson to learn that it isn't enough merely to practise with a great world champion.

Steve's painstaking preparation paid divi-dends. When he lifted the coveted trophy aloft at Sheffield in 1987 it marked his fourth win in six world championship finals there – an achieve-ment which speaks volumes for his character. A millionaire, he has wealth beyond even his wildest dreams, yet his sole motivation in life is to be No. 1, the best in the world and possibly the best of all time.

Steve knew from the minute he regained his crown that he would need to put in at least as much practice again in the following 12 months to have any chance of retaining the title.

There are too many young bloods in snooker for complacency to set in, as teenager Stephen Hendry has proved so often during his short, explosive rise to the top. The young Scot thinks nothing of practising eight hours daily at his manager Ian Doyle's club in Stirling. That may sound excessive, but look at the rewards he has collected already.

After Stephen's first championship win, in the Rothmans Grand Prix at Reading in 1987, beaten finalist Dennis Taylor, who like myself probably knows more about the early, thrilling days of Alex Higgins than anyone else, com-pared young Hendry to the great Irishman. 'But Stephen is doing in match-play what Alex was doing on the practice table,' said an admiring Dennis.

Yet Stephen leads as normal a life as pos-sible. He has a regular girlfriend and the same friends he had when he was at school. Snooker is obviously the dominant force in his life, but it isn't the be-all and end-all. To be able to drive around in an expensive BMW and live the life of a millionaire at the age of 19 demands sacrifices, however, and those sacrifices are made at the

table when his mates are maybe out on the town enjoying themselves. As Stephen has said: 'They all have to work for a living and in ten years time they'll still be doing the same job. I'll be able to retire and try something else then if I want to. And I'll be able to paint the town.'

For Willie Thorne potting balls is what snooker practice is all about. He prides himself on being Mr Maximum, the man who has made more 147s than anyone in the world. His tournament

Taylor-made for Hendry. Young Stephen gets the measure of Dennis at the start of their 1987 Rothmans Grand Prix final at Reading, which gave him his first major title.

PRACTICE MAKES PERFECT

HOW THE STARS PRACTISE

STRANGE LOGIC

'I knew I'd make one eventually in a match because I'd made 79 in practice.' – Willie Thorne on his 147 maximum during the 1987 Tennents UK championship

dreams came true at Preston in November 1987 when he made his first 147 in a match, during the Tennents UK Open. As luck would have it, the TV cameras weren't covering that stage of the event. Nevertheless, he chalked up maximum No. 80, and a few days later he added another one to his tally in practice.

While Willie is content to hammer in huge breaks every frame during practice sessions at his club in Leicester, his great pal Cliff Thorburn works diligently at honing his game to the standard he needs to maintain his top ten ranking. His form over the past seven years has fluctuated but, Davis apart, he is the most feared player on the circuit – no one takes liberties with him. Constant practice interspersed with frequent summer rounds of golf – he plays off a single handicap – more than compensate for the fact that Cliff isn't a natural stroke-maker like, for example, Jimmy White or Alex Higgins.

Terry Griffiths, one of the circuit's most consistent members, is also a dedicated player, practising on his own table at home in Llanelli for several hours daily throughout the season. Before joining the Matchroom stable he always took it easy during the summer months, but now he is involved in lengthy tours to the Far East and other far-flung places. The edge has gone from his game to a degree and the amiable Welshman admits that much of his time is now spent at the Terry Griffiths Matchroom Club, which is run by his wife, Annette, and eldest son Wayne.

He is the most gifted of players and as fluent as most, yet in recent years Terry has chopped and changed his cue action but without recapturing the rhythm that took him to the 1979 world championship at his first attempt.

In contrast to these great grafters, my old friend Dennis Taylor spent just an hour a day practising during his 1985 world championship

success. 'I'm cueing so well I don't need much more than a knock every day,' he told me midway through the tournament. Anyone who knows anything about the sport could see how well Dennis was playing in the build-up to that memorable final against Davis in which he came back from 8-0 down to win 18-17. And Dennis is getting better. An average period during the 1986-7 season was followed by some of the most spectacular snooker ever seen from one player. In a ten-week spell, Dennis picked up three overseas titles and the domestic Matchroom Champion of Champions at Southend, earning himself £172,000. He had hardly time to visit his family in Blackburn let alone practise. As I said before, when confidence is running high, anything is possible.

Poor Kirk Stevens looks a world-beater away from the bright lights of the television cameras, but in the last season or two his form has slumped as dramatically as his world ranking. Personal problems which spilled over into one or two of our least reputable newspapers did nothing to help his fading confidence and for a while he grew thoroughly disenchanted with the snooker scene. After an horrific start to the 1987/8 season when he bared his soul to TV presenter David Vine, the Canadian withdrew from the circuit in February 1988 for medical treatment in Toronto. At his best Kirk was good enough to push Jimmy White all the way in a memorable 1984 world semi-final, just months after becoming only the third player ever to make a 147 maximum on television.

Jimmy is another player who blows hot and cold over practice. Some days he'll play for hours on end, throughout the day and night, to bring his game to razor-sharpness. At other times he will just vanish – 'goes AWOL for two or three days', as his manager quaintly puts it. Before the 1986 world championship he took to jogging around the streets near his Wimbledon home with his dog to get fit for the Sheffield 17-day marathon. Alas, he bumped into a top-form Steve Davis in the quarter-finals and that was the end of the road for young Jim, who also fell to 'The Nugget' the following year.

Australian veteran Eddie Charlton seldom misses his daily 3-mile jog and such was his determination to regain a top 16 place in the rankings that he established a base in Britain in 1986 and his form took a turn for the better almost immediately.

Another fine performer on the practice table is funny-man John Virgo, whose brilliant impressions of the stars belie the fact that he is a world-class player. He looks absolutely unbeatable away from TV and every year he threatens to take a tournament apart but never quite makes it. He was known as the 'King of the North' as an amateur. I enjoyed a few healthy tussles with the Salford man in my early pro days. Nowadays he's a racehorse-owner, enjoying considerable success with his Jokist, but he can still be found most days keeping his game sharp at his local snooker centre in Guildford, Surrey, when he's not attending to the needs of the World Professional Billiards and Snooker Association, the sport's governing body, of which he was installed as chairman at the end of 1987.

With only nine frames deciding the qualifying rounds of all but two ranking tournaments, there is little margin for error. Every pro worth his salt knows he must be in shape right from the start of the season, and that can only mean one thing: practice. Barry Hearn's Matchroom squad are fortunate in that they are always involved in tough match-play tournaments around the world during the close season. On the other hand, too much tournament play can lead to staleness. I'm sure that some players, Terry Griffiths is a prime example, would much rather be spending their time at home relaxing with their families.

Many of our newer intake of professionals are attached to snooker centres as resident players. If they are fortunate enough to have some top-class amateurs in attendance, they are assured marvellous practice facilities. These players are the lifeblood of the pro-am tournaments which take place around the country throughout the year. It gives them invaluable match-play although few manage to take the top prizes, which range from anything up to £3,000 – not a fortune by major tournament standards, but manna from heaven for players not expecting to earn more than a few hundred pounds from the circuit.

Practice makes perfect – that's the theme of this chapter and that is what every youngster should strive to learn if he or she wants to make headway.

Incidentally, the 6 ft x 3 ft tables may seem a little childish to install at home, but they provide marvellous facilities for practice. You'd be surprised how much these small tables can help improve your game, and how much you can further your knowledge of cue-ball control, so don't underestimate their usefulness.

Over the top. Willie Thorne finds a way of bridging over the yellow to give him suitable contact on the cue ball. Note the splayed fingers, which allow him greater stability for the shot.

PERFECT SAFETY

GREAT EXPONENTS

Television audiences are accustomed nowadays to long bouts of safety from our more experienced professionals. They have been educated to accept that safety is an integral part of the modern game and, as such, can be just as fascinating as watching balls flying down pockets from all angles.

Who could ever forget the marvellous bouts of safety play between Dennis Taylor and Steve Davis in the 1985 world final at Sheffield, especially that heart-stopping sequence on the final black which saw the nerve-ends of both players screaming before Dennis potted the ball that would change his life.

Another great exponent of safety play is Cliff Thorburn. The greatest match it has ever been my pleasure to witness and commentate on was the world semi-final between the Canadian and Steve in 1986. I can't believe that the standard of snooker played in that match has ever been equalled – both men will be hard-pressed to reproduce such quality.

The two had met for the first time at Sheffield five years earlier when Thorburn was defending champion and Davis was the main challenger for his crown. On that occasion, Steve had weathered a great session by Thorburn, whose play had pinned the challenger to his chair for fully four frames, before Davis emerged triumphant.

Both men were older and wiser by 1986 and from the start the match promised to be something special. Davis had prophesied: 'The match will be a war.' His prediction was spot-on as the players swopped frame for frame in relentless fashion. Thorburn was only one frame adrift at the end of the first day (8-7) and so it continued until, at 12-12, Davis seemed to find an extra gear. The overdrive that separates Davis from the rest of the field on so many occasions gave

him four consecutive frames and a 16-12 win. Steve seemed on course for his fourth world title. However, the sheer physical and mental effort which he had expended during that 13½ - hour marathon told on him in the final. Steve was doubly unfortunate in that the semi-final finished late the night before the final began. A 24-hour breather before resuming battle would have been welcome, but that's snooker and even Steve wouldn't have it any other way. He looked a mere shadow at times against outsider Joe Johnson, who romped to a spectacular victory. It was a shock result, yet was not altogether surprising as Steve had put his heart and soul into beating Cliff to give him what he regarded as one of his most famous victories.

Both Steve and Ray Reardon have perfected the art of safety in snooker, rather like Muhammad Ali in boxing, whose basic instinct was to hit but not be hit. Ali escaped relatively unscathed for years although ultimately he paid the penalty for staying around too long. Today, Reardon, great champion though he was, is on the wane, but his vast knowledge of the angles and his ability to put an opponent under pressure by making him play from baulk rather than open up the game, still make him a dangerous player.

Another tremendous player is Rex Williams who is enjoying a new lease on a distinguished career that has spanned some 35 years. He forced his way into the world's top 16 for the first time in the 1986-7 season by virtue of some wonderful tournament play, including a 5-1 defeat of Steve Davis in the Rothmans Grand Prix on his way to his first final. Rex has consolidated his success, which has come rather late in his career. His main strengths have always been safety and weight of shot, which have been culled almost certainly from his vast billiards experience. A former world billiards champion, Rex has the uncanny knack of finding the exact angle when coming off one or two cushions and dropping on a red, or finding a pathway through to baulk when it would be easier to collide with the colours and leave the ball on. Some of his shots are totally foreign to the younger players, who never seem to consider playing those unusual kinds of shot. It may be that they don't have the ability to play them

CLOSE DECISION

'I'm a better player than Cliff. That is, I've beaten him so many times. But having said that, we are talking about fractions only.' – *Steve Davis on his great rivalry with Cliff Thorburn*

The 'Matchstick Man' in action. Cliff was given this nickname soon after his arrival in Britain in 1973 because he looked rather ungainly at the table. His tenacity and consistency are more than adequate recompense for any shortcomings as regards style, as his critics have been forced to admit. We can learn a little from every player.

and it is only later in their careers that they will have gained the necessary experience from the likes of Rex, Steve and Cliff.

Jimmy White was a wonderful potter as a youngster, arriving on the professional scene having won everything as an amateur. He lacked the knowledge at first to be a genuine force at the highest level but, today, after several years of competition against the great safety men, his game is on a par with theirs. This maturity in his game has slowed him down a little, perhaps because now he gives more thought to what he's doing and what he's hoping to achieve. Jimmy remembers the pots he

Mark of a genius. Stephen
Hendry has ruffled more than
a few snooker feathers while
still in his teens.

has missed; the best potter in the world, he thrives on being a winner, and tries to avoid making the same mistakes twice.

What is safety?

The secret of good play is to temper your natural ability with a little bit of safety in order to turn what could be a suicide pot into a safe shot, especially early in the game when such prudence could pay a handsome dividend. This approach will result in what is known as a percentage game.

The modern game is more attacking than it used to be, mainly because today's youngsters

PERFECT SAFETY

OPENING MOVES

ALL-ROUNDER

'I can play safety as well as anyone when I have to, but I'm an attacking player by nature. I love to play the shots and entertain.' – *Joe Johnson, after winning the 1986 world championship*

are weaned on potting, having followed the examples set by Alex Higgins, Willie Thorne and White. There are some wonderful break-builders around – one wonders sometimes how they will ever be beaten – but they do seem to lack experience, which only time and match-play will put right. Learn to find the right blend of potting and playing safe.

Opening moves

Most players probably aren't aware that safety play in fact starts with the very first stroke of the game. The player cueing off places the white ball in the D, or semi-circle, and attempts to hit the pack of reds without disturbing them too much. His aim is to get the cue ball back as close to the baulk cushion as possible, to leave the greatest distance between the white ball and the 15 reds, thus making his opponent's opening shot as difficult as possible. If he's failed to strike the cue ball properly, there's every chance he will have left a red which could give his opponent an opening right from the start. Where the safety skills of both players are of a high standard, a cat-and-mouse game could develop and it could take a while to produce a winner.

I've noticed over the past couple of years, from my vantage point in the television commentary box, that one or two of the younger professionals coming into the big tournaments are a little edgy. This is understandable when one considers that they are perhaps facing TV lighting and cameras for the first time and playing in an alien environment. The tendency is for them to break off rather sloppily, either failing to connect with the correct red ball or using too much side. As a result, the cue ball will sometimes strike the jaws of the corner pocket and come back into the reds or, in many instances,

the white will hit the blue on its way back towards baulk. Either way, the outcome invariably offers an early opportunity to the other player to get in among the balls. Constant practice should alleviate this problem, which can become a worry if it's not sorted out. The break-off itself is a defensive shot and you defeat its purpose if you allow your opponent a 'free shy at the coconut stall' as a result of your first shot.

A good opening shot could tempt your opponent into a mistake which could in turn allow you an early chance. Of course, you have to be aware of the need to return the ball to baulk in order to keep the pressure on at other times. When it isn't possible to negotiate a path back down the table – and sometimes it isn't – it may be necessary to keep the ball close to the top cushion. The skill for this particular shot comes from knowing that you are playing in the danger area, where the bulk of reds are lying, and having the strength of conviction to make the shot. It may necessitate your leaving the white behind a red and gambling that your opponent can't force an opening from it, or just keeping the white as tight as possible to the cushion, again to make things awkward.

Take, for example, a situation where there are 14 reds intact and one loose ball which has travelled to the other end of the table. Tit-for-tat play usually ensues with both players keeping the white as close to the pack as possible for fear of bringing the stray red into play. The ideal position for the white is behind the black ball on the cushion, making it even more difficult for your opponent because there is a limited target on the cue ball for him to strike. Invariably, his way out will be to dribble the ball into the pack of reds or, in the event of his being snookered behind black, to run the white off the cushion and alongside the pack, hoping for a touch without disturbing them.

Safety and confidence

There is another aspect to safety play which arises from situations where a player is tempted to have a go at potting a ball which will leave his opponent with the whole of the table for rich pickings should he miss. This is the time when a player must ask himself whether he feels confident enough to take the shot on or whether he wouldn't prefer to opt for safety. In other words, is it a percentage shot? Can he win or lose the frame from this one shot? A good safety shot can win a match, but to play a safety shot as an easy way out instead of attempting a pot is negative thinking. Confidence lies at the root of such decisions which depend on how well you are performing and, as important, how well your opponent is playing. There are no set rules to determine for you which shot you should choose. An 'attacking' safety stroke, with a snooker in mind, can be as vital as a pot.

Stephen Hendry, an outstanding potter, spent countless hours studying Steve Davis on video and came to the conclusion that he would need to concentrate more on safety in order to beat him. At his first opportunity he played even more safely than Steve to score a memorable first victory over the world champion.

Safety can be intriguing, but beginners should concentrate on learning to pot first. When playing against someone of the same standard you are hardly likely to lose the frame from one bad shot, as so often happens with the top professionals.

I used to be driven to distraction during my early days in the local billiard hall at Bacup by players obsessed with safety. All I wanted to do was pot balls and get on with the game, but I found myself caught in snookers all over the place. It was disheartening, and not a little depressing, being unable to go for shots, and not until my skills improved could I deal with them better and open up the game.

The double

An interesting feature of safety is the double, an unreliable shot that isn't seen too often in the pro game yet can be useful for sending the cue ball to safety or even potting the object ball for a bonus. A miss can leave you safe while a direct hit can lead to a frame-winning break. The only element of danger, and one players fear, is that the object ball heading for the pocket could hit the wrong side of the angle and travel back towards the white, leaving an easy target for the opponent (see diagram).

Professionals generally play the double as a 'shot to nothing'; it might be their only hope of continuing a break or finishing one on a safe

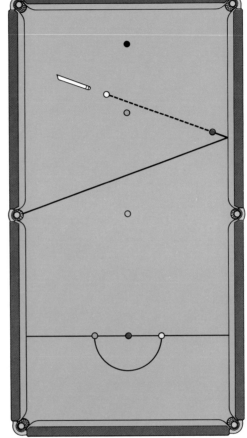

The double can be a useful shot to continue a break when all seems lost. It can be played with a degree of safety and should not be ignored when the situation arises.

note. The double should always be played with little power because the object ball rebounds at the reverse angle to which it travelled. The harder you hit the ball the more acute is its angle of departure. Because there is no direct target to aim for, you can never ascertain whether or not the shot has come off – it's another shot based on trial and error.

The easiest double is the one played into the middle pocket when the cue ball is fairly close to the opposite side cushion. It can also be played into a corner pocket but, because of the angle, most pros prefer to go instead for what is termed a 'cocked-hat double'; in fact it's a treble as the ball comes off three cushions and is aimed for a centre pocket (see diagram).

PERFECT SAFETY

BACK DOUBLE/COCKED-HAT DOUBLE

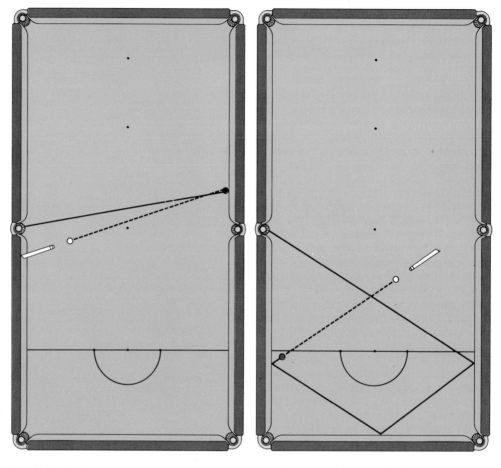

The back double is slightly trickier than the double as the cue ball is more difficult to control. The cue ball cannot be 'held' on a designated course, because it is played across the object ball.

The cocked-hat double is a variation of the double, but is actually a treble with the object ball being played off three cushions into a middle pocket. It can be a safety shot if you miss the pocket, but if you hit the angle of the pocket the object ball could cannon towards the opposite pocket or go back on itself.

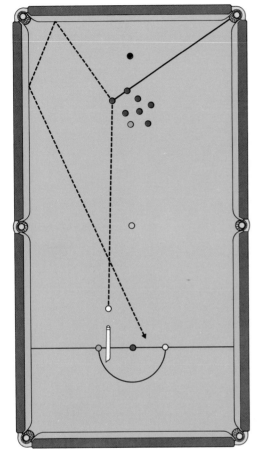

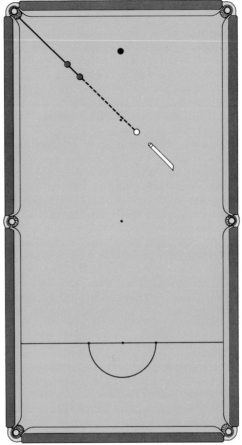

You will notice top class players use other unorthodox methods of potting a ball. One of these is the 'plant' or 'set', which is becoming a common manoeuvre in big-time snooker. By this method one red ball is used to pot another red. If the two reds are touching, the situation is generally called a 'set'; here, the white ball hits the first object ball to send the second into a pocket. The 'plant' is where the two reds are apart and the first one is played against the other to pot it. It is exciting and extremely effective if it comes off. However, the risk of missing and thereby leaving an easy shot for your opponent is high. Not always though, as the diagram on the left shows. Even if the second red doesn't go there is an easy escape route back to baulk. The diagram on the right highlights how simple a 'plant' can be. A simple screw shot is employed to bring the cue ball back a couple of inches for perfect position on the black and provide a good chance of capturing the last red.

SNOOKERS

AS MATCH WINNERS

Snooker, as I've stressed before, is very much like a game of physical chess. A thoughtful player will often work out a useful snooker to put his opponent in a lot of trouble. The same idea probably wouldn't even occur to another player, but situations are always there to be exploited and different players will find different ways of doing just that. There are all sorts of opportunities to be gained from laying a good snooker at the right time.

Snookers usually crop up where there are a couple of colours together or in close proximity. Let's imagine a situation (see diagram) where the brown and blue are fairly close together and the player at the table is 28 points behind with only the colours (worth 27 points) remaining. He needs a snooker. If he can manoeuvre the ball behind blue and brown, it would cover practically the entire margin of the table, especially if he can also send the yellow ball to the other end into the black spot area, thus giving his opponent all sorts of problems and himself, hopefully, every opportunity of winning the frame from this position.

Free balls

Another important aspect of snookers is the free-ball rule, which can be such an advantage to the man playing the snooker. It can turn a frame or even a match at a stroke because not only does your opponent concede a foul (at least four points) but you can take your pick of any ball on the table.

Let's assume this situation arises on the yellow ball. You'd pick up four points for the foul, plus another two for the free ball (the value of the yellow) and you'd still have all the colours to play with. So, from being perhaps 30 points behind with only 27 (the colours) left, you are now in the position of having a maximum of 33 points at your disposal.

Laying a snooker. The aim here is to bring the yellow behind the black, leaving the cue ball nestling behind blue and brown. Strike the white below centre for the desired stun effect.

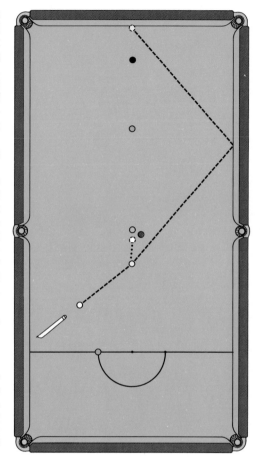

BAD TIMING

'I was born 30 years before my time. I'd have earned a fortune from snooker otherwise.' – *Cliff Wilson on the vast cash prizes available today*

Cliff Thorburn's mathematical brain worked overtime during the 1983 Benson and Hedges final at Wembley. He was some 60 points in arrears during an important stage of the match when he snookered Ray Reardon. Cliff played a perfect snooker and was sure he had earned a free ball when Ray missed. The referee thought otherwise but Cliff argued the point that he couldn't see either side of any red ball clearly and eventually persuaded the official to reverse his decision. From that point the Canadian cleared up brilliantly to steal the frame and went on to claim his second Masters title.

By coincidence Thorburn, the shrewdest of players, would be involved in a similar situation two years later when he played Jimmy White in

AS MATCH WINNERS

the 1985 Goya Matchroom final at Stoke. Jimmy led 7-0 after playing some of the most exhilarating snooker ever seen. He took a 74-point lead in frame eight and looked untouchable. Cliff needed at least three snookers. He secured two, earning a free ball from which he again cleared the table, halting Jimmy's march and setting himself up for what he later described as the best victory of his life. 'I can maybe make a maximum in a match again and I know I can win the world title again', he said, 'but I don't know whether I can ever repeat this performance.' By a strange quirk of fate Jimmy was to take his revenge in the most satisfying way some months later when the two players contested the Mercantile Credit Classic final at Warrington. This time Jimmy needed a snooker with just the pink and black remaining in the deciding frame

of a final which stood at 12-12. Thorburn looked to have won the match earlier in the frame when he opened up a 40-point lead, but choosing bravado rather than safety, foolishly he went for a difficult black pot along the top cushion and missed. The tension grew as White crept back into the picture inch by inch. With 15 points separating them White potted the blue ball and it looked as though he'd got his sums wrong, but his ice-cool brain had told him that if he could put Cliff in an awkward snooker he could steal the title. Jimmy played a perfect shot, sending the pink spinning to the centre of the table and leaving the cue ball behind the black. Even Cliff, with all his ability, failed to make contact, leaving the 'Wimbledon Whirlwind' two tough pots for his first major title. On such shots fame and fortune often depend, but they are unlikely to crop

Jimmy White is awkwardly placed for potting the black. Shots requiring great care and attention to detail demand the player's total concentration.

SNOOKERS

Which way did they go? Referee Len Ganley doesn't know, and Alex Higgins is just as puzzled.

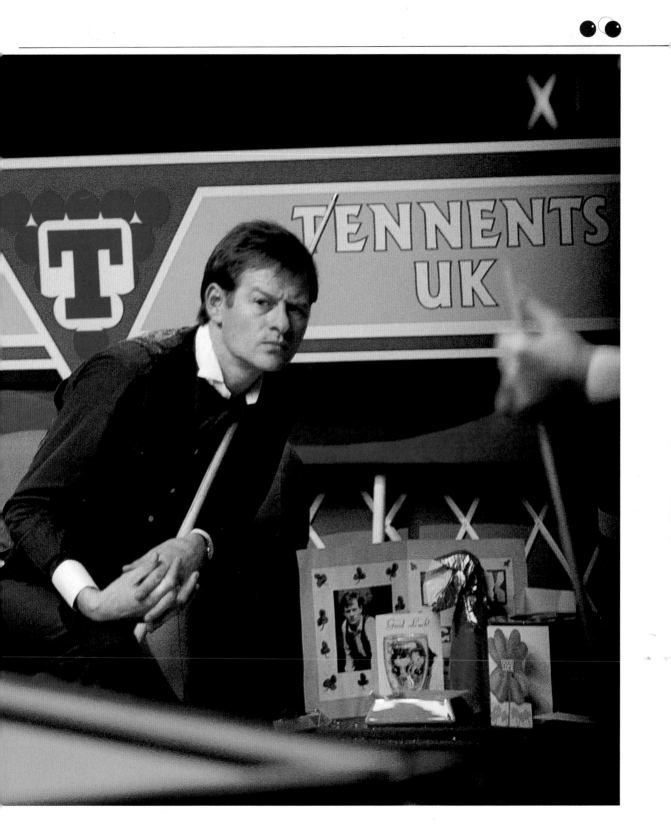

ESCAPE ROUTES

up during club matches because the skill required of the player is so high. They do, however, demonstrate the value of snookers and free balls.

Escape routes

A healthy knowledge of angles is obviously required for dealing with snookers, especially those where the cue ball and object ball are some 10 to 12 ft apart with a few other balls lying between.

1. Study the diagram and imagine you are the player snookered in the baulk area. To extricate yourself you need to strike the red close to the top cushion but in such a way that you don't leave your opponent on the other available red.

2. Here is another situation which requires your escape back into baulk by coming off the main bunch of reds. The ball must be struck perfectly, sliding off the edge of the pack in order for the cue ball to return to the baulk area without too much damage. If the shot is played incorrectly, the reds could be struck too thick, spreading them more and leaving the cue ball in the danger zone for an opponent to clear up.

A golden rule I learned a long time ago is, avoid sending the object ball towards a pocket when attempting to lay a snooker. Otherwise you would leave an easy pot for your opponent should the snooker not materialize, and that would turn a good opportunity into a huge disadvantage.

3. Cushions can be a great advantage when escaping from snookers, as shown in the diagram. There is one red left on the table, close to the black. The plan is to get out of trouble, keep the red safe and create your own snooker. The contact must be spot-on, so aim to hit the top cushion first, which will bring the white to hit the back of the red, leaving the cue ball somewhere around the black area and sending the red ball down into baulk.

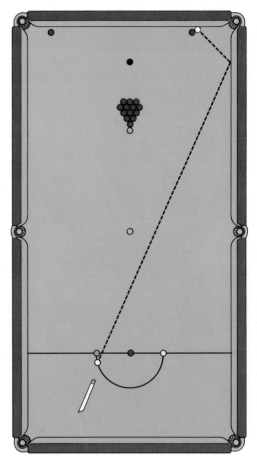

Escape route 1: This is a plain-ball shot requiring direction, pace and correct contact. Drop on to the red and cover the other red at the opposite corner pocket.

DAVIS REACHES THE PARTS . . .

'Steve Davis is No. 1 because he wins frames other players can't win.' – *Jimmy White after losing the classic 1987 Tennents UK final*

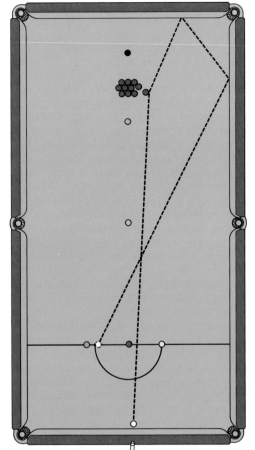

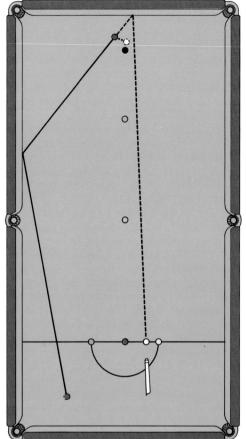

Escape route 2: To escape from this snooker and return to baulk, you need pace on the ball and a wide angle. Strike the ball firmly, applying left-hand side.

Escape route 3: Using the cushion to turn the tables on your opponent. In this instance, the cue ball comes off the top cushion for full ball contact on the red, sending the red back to baulk and leaving the cue ball virtually behind the black. The shot required is played with strong left-hand side.

COMPETING WITH PRESSURE

THE MODERN GAME

8

Snooker is competitive at all levels today, even when it is played at home on miniature tables. The gap between professionals and top amateurs, once a huge divide, has lessened somewhat in recent years with the advent of full-time 'players', who aren't necessarily professionals but have sponsors and earn a comfortable living from the flourishing pro-am circuit which exists around the country.

Tony Drago earned some £9,000 in 15 months before accepting pro status. Martin Clark, the West Midlands youngster who broke into big-time snooker in 1987 with a shock win over world No. 3 Neal Foulds and an even more stunning 5-0 whitewash of 1985 world champion Dennis Taylor on his TV début, was said to have made £22,000 during his last season as an amateur. Amazingly, only 26 players in the world accumulated more prize money than Clark; even New Zealander Dene O'Kane, who reached the Embassy world championship quarter-finals, was behind him in earnings.

Clark won't always have it so easy, but the fact that he was able to win his first seven tournament matches as a professional underlines how impressive the top amateurs are today.

Joe Davis considered that a player had to complete a 15-year apprenticeship before he could be accepted as a fully fledged professional. Jimmy White's success in the world amateur championship at the age of 18, and Stephen Hendry's acceptance as a pro at only 16 then victory in a major ranking tournament two years later, stands that ancient theory on its head.

Television has helped enormously in the development of the game and in improving the standard of play among youngsters. Twenty years ago eager novices would have had to rely on a more experienced player at their club or local billiard hall to point out their faults. There was little or no televised snooker. The occasional glimpses of Joe Davis in grainy black and white, sandwiched between other Saturday afternoon sports programmes, was the best they could hope for. Now there are resident coaches at most reputable snooker centres who are ready and willing to encourage any young man or woman with talent. The current favourable conditions greatly benefit those

talented enough to take advantage of them, hence the phenomenal rate at which today's youngsters learn the game.

To be fair, snooker was in its infancy when Joe Davis launched, and won, the first world championship in 1927. It received little media attention for many years. Even when Alex Higgins caused a sensation by winning the world title at his first attempt, as a 22-year-old in 1972, his triumph was largely ignored by the national press. One of the popular papers carried a paragraph recording the event, but that, I believe, was the extent of media interest. Today, yards of column inches are devoted to snooker's most prestigious tournament and to the players, who have become household names and folk heroes in the space of a decade.

More important, from a beginner's point of view, are the video recordings which are now available. These enable the enthusiast to study at length the styles and playing habits of all the champions, so much so that it would be almost possible to learn how to play the game without ever picking up a cue. A slight exaggeration perhaps, but the power of television as a learning medium should not be underestimated.

For every Jimmy White and Steve Davis, however, there are literally millions of people who will never progress beyond the confines of their local club. That's not to say such players can't improve their standard and gain additional satisfaction from the game, just that they may not wish to put in the extra effort it takes to play well. Snooker doesn't have to be serious and all-demanding. For many it has become something of a family sport and as such can be enormous fun. Women are now made welcome at most snooker centres, whereas the old billiard hall was regarded as a male-only preserve. Girls like Allison Fisher, Stacey Hillyard and Ann Marie Farren, all world champions in their own right, are regular century break-makers and are beginning to make an impact on the men's game.

Making your way

A player needs to be gifted to move away from club-level snooker and into the inter-club leagues, where 100-break players are commonplace. If you are keen to try there's no

Playing it straight – dignity and industry. All players have their own methods of keeping pressure at bay, as Davis and White demonstrate during their breathtaking 1987 Tennents UK final.

reason why you shouldn't test your ability on the amateur or pro-am circuits once you have the confidence. First, though, find a comfortable level at which to play – it's not always that easy. It is almost impossible to categorize snooker players from the learner stage, which seems to be a phenomenon unique to snooker. With football, for instance, you can state with a fair amount of certainty that most kids who play will be of similar standard and so can be organized into teams and leagues according to age. True, there will be the odd player who stands out, perhaps one in every team, but the other lads will still be able to enjoy themselves playing with or

against him. Imagine coming up against a 13-year-old Jimmy White across a snooker table! Both Jimmy and his close school friend Tony Meo were scoring centuries and playing big money matches all around the London area at that age. Legend has it that Jimmy once borrowed £100 from his father, Tommy, and returned it the same day with a £900 bonus.

Today there are hundreds of children all over the United Kingdom capable of marvellous displays of snooker expertise. A 12-year-old, Ian Scanlon, knocked in an age-group world record 131-break at Ilford Snooker Centre in Essex in October 1987 and missed a simple black for a

COMPETING WITH PRESSURE

PRESSURE: POSITIVE/NEGATIVE

BREAD, BUTTER – AND JAM

'Even the easiest of shots can be missed when the pressure is on. But the great players miss fewer.' – *John Virgo on why those bread-and-butter pots don't always go down*

138 total clearance. How could he possibly play in an under-13 team and benefit?

Because snooker is an individual sport, youngsters quickly find their own level, whether it be with adults or other children of the same age, and work out which direction to take from there. What is important for the aspiring snooker player is that he (or she) should be a member of a club that is affiliated to the Billiards and Snooker Control Council, which runs the amateur game. The B&SCC is responsible for all the official junior and adult championships held each year, and it is through these competitions that most of our household names first made a reputation for themselves. These national competitions provide an excellent apprenticeship; Ray Reardon, John Spencer, Terry Griffiths and Jimmy White are just some of the names on the English Amateur Championship trophy who went on to bigger things. Rex Williams was British under-16 champion in 1948 and 1949, a title which Stephen Hendry won 34 years later. Willie Thorne, Mike Hallett, White and Virgo were also junior champions. A host of stars are former winners of the British under-19 title, including Dean Reynolds, Neal Foulds, Tony Meo and Tony Knowles.

To reach that standard you have to have talent. There are no class barriers in snooker: if you are good enough you will progress, it's as simple as that. Dozens of open events take place throughout the UK and these are the testing grounds. It's probably as hard on the pro-am circuit as it is among the professional qualifying tournaments because there are so many full-time players hoping to achieve the great breakthrough into the pro ranks. To become a professional you must first prove your worth in a series of pro-ticket tournaments, run by the World Professional Billiards and Snooker

Association (the game's ruling body), in conjunction with various major sponsors and the B&SCC. From these events the top eight, plus the English and world amateur champions, graduate to play-off against the bottom ten professionals each year on a promotion-relegation basis.

There is no short-cut to progress at snooker. You will soon find your level and enjoy playing at that standard. You've either got what it takes or you haven't, but either way you can still enjoy the game to the full. Hopefully, you will be able either to improve your game or make real headway after reading this book. The game isn't just about Steve Davis and co. and it isn't just about winning, but it must surely help to have a better understanding of what you are trying to achieve . . . and how to go about it.

A positive attitude is essential, however well you progress, and there is no substitute for experience. A bad shot which may have cost you dearly early on in your career should be remembered and remedied should the same position occur again.

Pressure: positive and negative

Professional players have in many ways spoiled snooker for armchair-watchers with ambitions to play. They have made the game look so easy and comfortable. That impression is misleading and doesn't reflect what really goes on in the close confines of a playing area, which could be likened to a snakepit or gladiator's arena, such is the intensity and fierceness of contest.

The word 'professional' suggests being top of the class. There is a lot of pressure on players, from Davis downwards, to do well, and the knowledge that they are performing in front of an audience of millions makes them want to please. The last thing a player wants is to make a fool of himself or herself in front of friends or family and this fear increases the pressure.

By wanting to win so badly players may do themselves a disservice and not perform to their own high standards. Getting the mixture right – by relaxing, not trying too hard and keeping a clear head to work out situations – is not easy, as countless professionals will testify.

There are no second chances in snooker, unlike golf where you can shrug off one bad shot

Concentration and grit are the main assets that have kept Cliff Thorburn among the top seeds for several years.

with a 100-yard walk and even take out your frustration on your caddie before getting a second chance to put matters right. One mistake and you may have to sit for ten minutes and watch your opponent take full advantage by potting all the balls you had lined up for yourself.

There comes a time in every snooker player's career when he reaches what I would term the panic level stage: nothing the player attempts goes right and he seems incapable of playing himself out of danger. The task then – and it's very difficult – is to think constructively and work out what needs to be done to find a safety zone.

That type of pressure occurs all the time in snooker and intensifies because you know the TV cameras will be on you at some stage and you daren't show emotion. You sit there, willing the opponent to miss and give you another bite at the cherry, but your expression can't reflect that desire. There is pressure, too, on your opponent to take full advantage of your error.

Pressure comes in various forms and whether those forms are negative or positive depends on the player's level of confidence. Someone with a temperament like Steve Davis will revel in pressure if his confidence is running high. There have been many instances in the past where Steve has transmitted as well as received pressure. Then it's all down to a battle of willpower and nerve.

Snooker history abounds with stories of players 'cracking' under pressure – even Davis himself, when his failure to pot an awkward but sinkable final black led to Dennis Taylor's historic 1985 world championship victory. In that match all the pressure had been applied by Steve in the early stages when he opened up an 8-0 lead. Dennis, by coming back at him strongly in the second session to be only 9-7 behind, then continually dogging him throughout the second day, eventually reversed the pressure so that he had nothing to lose and everything to gain. Steve was the overwhelming favourite to win, yet his confidence drained the longer the match went on.

I remember another time, in Australia, when that great veteran warrior Eddie Charlton felt the tension so much that he screamed at the top of his voice, which must have frightened the audience.

COMPETING WITH PRESSURE

Clap hands here comes Joe Johnson. But he lost his world crown in 1987 after a gallant bid against Steve Davis.

Davis himself admits: 'We all crack if the pressure is too fierce. We wouldn't be human if we didn't.' He will almost certainly recall the green ball that got away against Willie Thorne in the semi-final of the 1985 Mercantile Credit Classic at Warrington. Willie had opened up a sizeable lead in the final frame of a real nail-biter only for Steve to play himself into such a position that an easy snooker behind the brown would have put him in with a good chance. Instead, Steve tried a risky green to the middle pocket, missed and tossed the match away.

At the same venue three years earlier Tony Meo had needed a simple yellow off the spot, then the rest of the colours, not only to beat Steve for the first time in his pro career but to pocket his first major trophy. Alas, a supporter shouted 'Come on Tony' and his concentration wavered long enough for him to miss the pot. As Steve said: 'He should have got up off the shot and started again.' The title meant so much to Tony and, sadly, he's still searching for that elusive big win.

Steve staged his greatest comeback when he rallied from 13-8 down against Willie Thorne in the 1984 Coral UK final at Preston. Willie was coasting to a famous victory on a series of massive breaks and there was little Steve could do but sit back and admire the show.

Suddenly, Willie wobbled, missing an easy blue into the centre pocket which would have made it 14-8 and put him two frames from home. Steve climbed down from the gallows and, though the pressure was still intense because he couldn't afford to give Willie another chance, proceeded to turn the match slowly but surely for what he has described as one of the most satisfying victories of his career. When you consider the dozens of titles he's won, that really is saying something.

Cliff Thorburn was the victim of mental pressure he exerted on himself in a famous Coral UK semi-final against Alex Higgins at Preston. The Canadian, who had snookered himself behind the pack of reds, nominated the green and made contact. To his dismay the referee called 'foul' and even though TV microphones and many spectators heard Thorburn clearly, the official refused to be swayed. Thorburn stormed from the arena, then returned to ask Higgins to

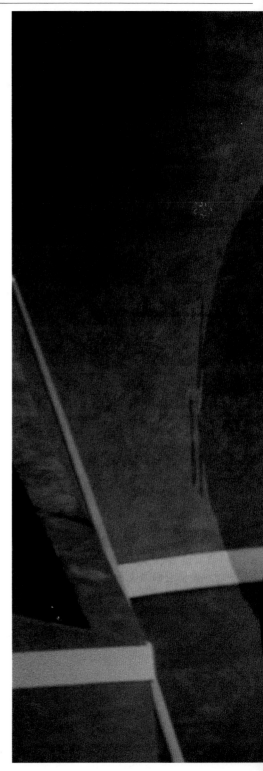

COMPETING WITH PRESSURE

PRESSURE: POSITIVE/NEGATIVE

back him up. Alex said he hadn't seen or heard the incident and refused to get involved. Cliff replied: 'In that case you can't use this,' indicating the extension he'd allowed Alex to share.

The match had been nicely balanced until that moment, but Thorburn was so wound up by the decision that he threw the match away. If he'd looked at it logically, he'd have seen that Alex, who went on from that stroke to make a frame-winning break, would have been in the same position anyway whether or not Thorburn had been penalized.

I was commentating on the match and afterwards I drove Cliff back to the hotel where, believe it or not, we shared a bacon and egg sandwich and a bottle of champagne. I told him I thought he should have steadied himself when he left the arena then asked for an official ruling from the senior tournament referee. Even if the official in charge hadn't heard the call, Cliff would have received support from the spectators to back up his claim. Cliff admitted he hadn't been thinking along those lines because he was so incensed by the decision.

Perhaps the most famous – or infamous – example of pressure came in the 1979 State Express World Team Cup when Patsy Fagan, once regarded as the finest amateur of all, froze when using the rest and couldn't play the shot. The Irishman suffered agonies for months afterwards, and though he went on to overcome the 'yips', he was never the same player again.

The game is littered with instances of 'if only'. Both John Parrott and Tony Drago have had cause to regret careless or hurried shots against Davis in past seasons. Drago, the exciting young Maltese player, had given Davis all sorts of problems in their 1986 Tennents UK Championship quarter-final. When he opened with a 54 break in the last frame he seemed home and dry. Davis, as he does so often, clawed his way

GRIM PERSPECTIVE

'Every time I look down my cue I see a nightmare.' – *Kirk Stevens during the worst period of his career, as he tumbled down the rankings in 1987*

back into contention only to hand his rival a gilt-edged opportunity on the colours. All Tony needed was the easiest of yellows off its spot then a straight clear-up to see off the world No. 1. Instead of composing himself before lining up the shot, he jumped from his chair like a scalded cat, snatched at this chance of glory and bodged it.

John Parrott was in a similar situation against Steve in the Mercantile final at Blackpool a year later. On that occasion he had come from a long way behind to lead 11-10. With only two frames needed he missed a short red along the cushion and barely got another shot as the world champion notched up three big breaks to win 13-11. Two weeks later Parrott blew it again, this time against Mike Hallett in the Benson & Hedges semi-final. Leading by 41 points with only the colours remaining he slammed the green ball off the table, giving Hallett the tiniest of escape routes. Parrott's confidence evaporated as Hallett reversed the pressure and secured the three snookers he needed for victory.

Another form of pressure can stem from financial worries. Not every player who comes into the game is fortunate enough to have a sponsor. Unknowns have no means of support other than prize money, so every shot, every frame and every match becomes vital. The pressure imposed by such circumstances could work in one of two ways. It could either inspire the player to excel or panic him into performing badly. Victory leads automatically to success and endorsement spin-offs, but the worry of having to survive on prize money could weigh very heavily indeed.

Pressure actually goes hand in hand with concentration and a player's mind can be diverted by the opponent rather than giving 100 per cent attention to the game itself and the way the balls are spread.

Pressure or tenseness can lead to a 'tightening' and a loss of timing and discipline – the rigid pattern needed to perform to maximum potential. The player's brain speeds up but doesn't react with its usual precision. The physical effects of pressure often show in the face: the eyes redden or the cheeks become flushed, and perspiration appears. The key is to slow the brain down to regain the subtleness required.

Fancy that! Dapper Rex Williams (left) with pool wizard Steve 'Pinky' Mizerak and Steve 'Flat Cap' Davis during their snooker-pool challenge series. Such events allow the most unlikely players to reveal a lighter side.

COACHING JUNIORS
THE SANDELL METHOD

It was my good fortune some years ago to meet a character who has as much, if not more, enthusiasm for snooker as I have. I had pursued the sport from an early age through the local billiard hall at Bacup in my native Lancashire, to Blackburn's famed Benarth, or Post Office Club as it was called, where I shared some happy years with both Alex Higgins and Dennis Taylor. We lived for the game: Alex would practise for ten, even twelve hours daily; Dennis and I not quite so diligently (because we had to earn a living outside snooker) but with as much passion as the Hurricane.

I didn't think anyone could rival our keenness until I befriended Frank Sandell. I had met him at a few championships where we chatted about coaching and the game in general, but did not get to know him well until I was invited to help launch a brand new snooker club in Worthing. Frank, who lived just outside this seaside town, discovered I was to be the resident coach at the club and offered his services. He had given up a successful job in the construction industry some years before in order to devote all his energies to the game, so he was no ordinary fan. Now he deals in equipment, has a vast collection of memorabilia and is a full-time coach.

By the end of the club's first day, in December 1981, we had enrolled only four members, and it looked as though a genteel Sussex resort mainly populated by retired people was hardly the right environment to further the emerging snooker boom. Six months later the Connaught Club, as it was known, was bursting at the seams, so we must have done something right.

What helped, undoubtedly, were the junior coaching sessions Frank and I introduced on Saturday mornings for locals. Through this scheme, I'm proud to say, we 'discovered' Allison Fisher at the age of 13. Within the space of five years she became the finest woman player there has been. Naturally gifted as a player, it wasn't long before we were using her as a role model whenever we wanted to demonstrate particular facets of the game.

Frank's reputation as a coach is spreading but his positive ideas on how youngsters should be coached deserves a wider appreciation. Since those days at the Connaught Frank has moved across the road to the New Central

Snooker Club, which is owned and run by Sue Kelly, daughter of the famed Ted Zanoncelli whose Zans Club in Tooting nurtured both Tony Meo and Jimmy White. He runs his Frank Sandell Schools from this base. At any given time the 200 or so youngsters in his charge there and at other clubs in the area can recite the Sandell gospel. The initials of his club, FSS, are also the initials of the philosophy upon which he has founded his coaching clinics: Friendship, Sportsmanship and Skill. Those qualities will stand any youngster in good stead throughout his sporting life, whether or not he or she excels.

It is important that good snooker habits are instilled in youngsters from an early age and Frank, who has advised and encouraged both myself and my co-author throughout the writing of this book, has agreed to contribute the following section on junior coaching.

It is my belief that every child interested in playing snooker should have a working knowledge of billiards and that every coach should have a totally comprehensive knowledge of that game.

A coach isn't necessarily a highly skilled player, but if he is working with young people he must be able to answer ALL their questions. Youngsters are more demanding, have more inquiring minds and have a greater thirst for learning than adults I've coached. Kids ask questions. Coaches must have the answers; the moment they can't come up with them, they have lost credibility.

I'm a firm believer in using billiards as a successful platform from which to teach snooker, so every child who comes to me for coaching must learn to play billiards first. Some youngsters may not like the game – to be honest, many of them don't – but they have no option if they want to learn with me. Billiards is valuable for several reasons: the billiard table is uncluttered and allows free cueing; a billiard stroke will more easily reveal where a child is going wrong technically; and billiards allows you to demonstrate clearly how one ball will react when it hits another.

There is nothing sweeter than demonstrating how one ball curves off another as a natural reaction. Jimmy White plays the most amazing shots that leave the cue ball swerving all over the

Little and large – Big Jim Bernadine and Little Lee Weston, both Frank Sandell pupils. Lee's cue is actually a fraction longer than the one used by Jim, which just goes to show that there are no hard and fast rules for choosing cues.

COACHING JUNIORS
THE BASICS

**Looking down the line of fire.
Stephen Hendry is parallel as
possible with the bed of the
table. To adopt this stance,
Stephen has a pronounced
dip in his back.**

place. All the kids believe he does this by putting side on the white, but half the time the balls are reacting naturally. I don't suppose even Jimmy knows why. He's probably hitting the ball very close to the centre and creating enormous curves because of the tremendous power he's generating through the shot as one ball comes off another.

One reason why I've had some success as a coach is that I can appreciate fully how difficult it is to play the game. I've never found snooker easy, and after 30 years I'm still not the player I want to be. I can play all the shots, of course, but in isolation. I've never had the ability to string shots together in the manner of a Jim Meadowcroft or any of his fellow-professionals (or the top amateurs for that matter), so I've not been able to match their achievements. However, what I have managed to do is find an effective way of communicating the theory and practice of the game, which is the most important part of teaching any sport. I coach my juniors to coach themselves. I pass on to them sufficient knowledge and basic exercises for them to teach themselves. Jim has used the phrase 'trial and error' throughout this book, and I can't think of a better way to describe the learning process.

Getting the basics right

Children need to understand what is going wrong and for what reason, and they need to have an idea of how they can correct their errors. There are a few basics they should check out first. Timing is a key factor in snooker and is the most likely cause of error when children are playing below par. Check the amount of grip in the back hand. How tight is it? Where is the hand on the cue? A player's mental approach is of crucial importance too. If you are feeling 'tight' mentally, you'll be 'tight' physically. I encourage all my players – juniors and adults alike – to take a deep breath as they approach the table, especially when a game is not going to plan. The breath should be released slowly as you sink down into the shot and you should feel your neck and shoulders relax. This approach won't necessarily work for every player – no single approach ever does - but it should help.

The stance will vary from player to player, because people vary in their height and build.

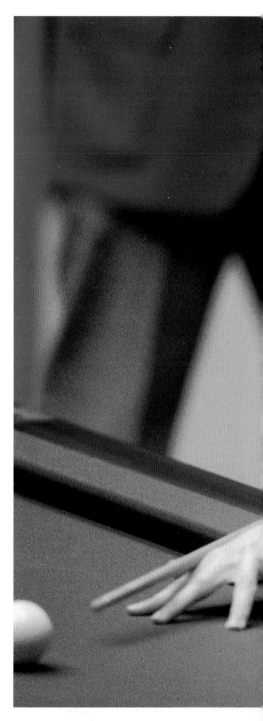

Queuing up for the cue master. Jimmy White signing autographs for fans during the 1987 Matchroom Championship at Westcliff. Players' activities are not confined to the snooker table these days.

COACHING JUNIORS
THE BASICS

THE EQUALIZER

'The game has been made easier for the potters and harder for the more skilful players because the pockets are bigger now.' – *Tony Knowles*

What is imperative for every player is total stillness of the head on the shots.

One method of hammering home the basic principle of stillness is by demonstrating that for most snooker shots, you don't have to bend over the table, even if you are very tall. By allowing your left hip (assuming you are right-handed) to come in towards the cue slightly, you will find you lower your height automatically and are pulled into the shot. Steve Davis is a classic example of a tall man who looks perfectly comfortable at the table. He never bends into a shot, rather lowers himself to the table. If you are tall and find it uncomfortable to play snooker, it is almost certainly because you are bending and so putting pressure on the curve of your spine lower down. By lowering yourself you can still keep the back leg straight, although that isn't imperative. It makes sense, though, because it keeps the body firm. What is essential is that you don't relax the joints when down on the shot because you would be liable to wobble. Dennis Taylor hardly keeps his right leg straight, but I don't suppose he was worrying too much about having a slight kink in his knee when he won the 1985 world championship. Going down through the line of aim with your head up is the secret, so that you don't suddenly thrust it up once you are on the shot and distort your view of the object ball. Look at Stephen Hendry (see photograph on p.73): his neck is like a giraffe's but his head is always up and looking through the line of aim straight away.

Part of the reason for Steve Davis's success is that he is very tall and has a long reach so he can eliminate many shots others have to play with the rest. However, being tall has its pitfalls, certainly at the beginner stage. Little Lee Weston, one of my bright young pupils who had a 39-break to his credit at the age of seven, is the perfect model to demonstrate my theories.

Like all small kids playing snooker, he is best when stretched slightly. He can only pull the cue back a little way otherwise he couldn't reach the ball, so the shortened backswing gives him more accuracy when he hits the ball. Children can't send the cue all the way through the ball, so they can't get the variety of shot they will develop as they grow. What they can get, though, is a good, clean strike on the object ball, which is very important.

Enjoying the game

The first point I make to youngsters looking for guidance is that they should enjoy themselves. I don't worry too much about coaching them at the start, and even before they've picked up a cue I make them understand the fun that can be had from the game. My object is to teach them to teach themselves to play, but if they don't get any fun out of that then there's no real point in taking up snooker.

My main complaint with some parents is that they expect their children to be world-beaters. I stress to them all: don't come to me with your ten-year-old and demand that I make him a champion. Even the world's greatest coach would find that an impossible task. By the same token, I can't guarantee that promising 14-year-olds can be transformed into champions. What these youngsters will get through me and, hopefully, any reputable coach, is the pleasure that comes from taking part in and being fulfilled by the game. I teach the kids in groups so that they can help and encourage each other.

I run a regular series of junior handicap tournaments in my area. Nothing gives me greater pleasure than the sight of an older boy drawn against a little one actually stopping in mid-frame and demonstrating how a particular shot should be played. When you can generate that sort of spirit between young players, you know you are beginning to achieve something really worthwhile.

Some parents, and even the kids themselves, don't appreciate fully that there is no magic wand. 'My son is a champion and I want you to make him into an even bigger one', is the usual plea. More often than not, though, I am approached by sensible parents of children who want to learn how to play the game.

Problems

Inconsistency causes more heartache than any other problem in snooker, especially when a player's knowledge of the game and ability to play it are developing. My advice is that given by all responsible coaches: look first at your timing and your final sighting of the shot. However, when a young player experiences a sudden loss of form or ability, the physical process of growing is a likely explanation. Many players aged between 8 and 18 will suffer 'growing pains', which manifest themselves as irregular discomfort on the shot, lack of coordination and, often, changes in temperament. In these circumstances, a coach can suggest minor adjustments to the player's stance to help ease the technical difficulties, but there is little else he can do of a practical nature. Where temperament is concerned, an explanation of what 'growing up' means and the emotional turmoil that results from the body's changes should reassure the young player that his ability has not deserted him forever. A constructive, sympathetic approach on the part of the coach should dispel any fears and free the youngster to concentrate on playing the game and, most important of all, enjoying it once again.

Points to remember

A coach's basic function is to speed the learning curve but, as I stressed earlier, he's got to have all-round knowledge and he mustn't be pedantic. Youngsters and adults come in all shapes and sizes, so there has to be a certain amount of flexibility. I use all sorts of slogans to help players remember good habits.

Play the balls and not the pockets

We all know where the pockets are so line of aim is the main concern. When it's a straight pot the line of aim is through the centre of the white ball, through the centre of the object ball and to the back of the pocket. If you move that aim a millimetre either side, the line changes and you won't pot the ball. Sight through the cue as though you were aiming a gun, pause at the final backswing then 'fire' it.

There is hardly a player in the game who doesn't pause at the end of the backswing. It is vital because it allows your eyes to go forward through the line of aim, to adjust and focus, and your brain to tell your arm to stop coming back and start going forward.

You get nothing for rushing

This is a standard Frank Callan saying, and if it's good enough for the man the professionals turn to for advice . . . A hurried shot is a wasted one, as we have seen so often on TV, even by the big boys. Study Davis next time he is faced with a crunch shot. He always takes a deep breath and takes in the situation before committing himself, even for what appears to be a simple pot.

Stop at the back and give it a crack

Simple word associations can help coach a youngster into good habits. This one has to do with the pause again. Using Davis again as a model, watch how he pauses deliberately on all his shots, and stays down long after the cue ball and the object ball have travelled their respective courses.

Overcoach is overkill

A coach who curbs a player's natural ability will eventually kill off that ability. There's more to life than squeezing an extra few pounds out of a pupil rather than sending him on his way with enough knowledge for him to be able to work out things for himself as well as express his ideas freely on the table.

Set targets

This is perhaps the most important advice for practising. Routines can be the most boring part of learning and maintaining standards, but they needn't be. Make a game of it and challenge yourself to beat targets you set before the start of each session. You'll be surprised how determined you become.

TALENT SPOTTER

'He will be there or thereabouts for as long as he wants to be.' – former world champion John Pulman on Steve Davis who, in 1980, when this prophesy was made, had still to win his first tournament.

AFTERTHOUGHTS

When Jim Meadowcroft asked me to 'ghost' his book *Higgins, Taylor and Me* I was flattered to say the least. We had been great pals for years, but until we began working on the project I had no idea of his vast knowledge, not just of the players but of the game itself.

I was asked to produce a simple instruction book on the game shortly after the 1987 world championship. It required just a telephone call to the Rossendale Valley in Lancashire and a short conversation to 'sign' my expert.

'What the heck do you know about playing the game?' asked Middlepocket, as Jim is known affectionately on the circuit. 'Nothing,' I replied. 'That's why I'm calling you.'

In fact, we make an ideal combination. Jim was such a natural player in his youth that he never experienced the traumas of most average club players; potting and controlling the cue ball with spin held few mysteries for him. But I suffered agonies as a youngster wondering why I couldn't make the ball screw back, and why I could never pot more than a couple of balls in succession.

Whenever Jim explained a particular technique, I was able to tell him of all the pitfalls most play-for-fun enthusiasts have encountered along the way. For years his great forte as a BBC snooker summarizer and lately as an ITV commentator has been the simple way he describes the big-time action to millions of viewers. In the same way he was able to put across to me all the basic techniques necessary to get satisfaction from what has become the nation's No.1 spectator and participant sport. In a short while Jim had me screwing the ball back a couple of feet without fear of damaging the precious cloth.

That's not to say I'll ever be able to play the game to any great standard, but the thrill of actually being able to stun and screw properly for the first time, and occasionally seeing the white ball going where I want it to, more than makes up for 30 years of frustration on the snooker table.

My job has been merely to assemble Jim's thoughts and put them into words, but even that task wouldn't have been possible without advice from another great mutual friend, Frank Sandell, whose junior coaching clinics are the talk of the south coast. Frank was able to simplify matters even further from a junior angle. I believe, all in all, we have produced a book which will be of great benefit to any snooker newcomer.

HENNESSY

ANGLED Cue ball is obstructed by a corner of the cushion, preventing a direct stroke to any balls 'on', as demonstrated brilliantly by Alex Higgins against Steve Davis in the 1987 Tennents UK Championship.

BALL MARKER Plastic accessory which enables referee to mark exact position of ball removed for cleaning or any other reason.

BALL ON Any ball which can be struck fairly by the cue ball.

BAULK The area at the bottom of the table, including the 'D' from which a player cues off at the start of a frame and after an in-off.

BAULK CUSHION The cushion at the bottom end of the table.

BREAK A number of pots made in succession: red-colour, red-colour, etc.

CENTRE SPOT Midway between top and bottom cushions. The blue ball sits on this spot.

CLEARANCE When all the balls on the table have been potted, leaving only the white.

CUE A wooden implement of ash or maple used to play snooker.

CUE BALL The white ball which is struck by the cue to pot other balls.

DOUBLE The art of playing the object ball against a cushion and rebounding it into an opposite pocket.

FOUL This is committed when a player fails to strike the correct object ball, misses altogether or goes in-off.

FREE BALL This is awarded after a foul shot if the object ball cannot be sighted clearly. There must be an entire ball-width of space either side of the intended object ball, otherwise the striker is entitled to elect any ball on the table to substitute for the value of the ball on. Thus, the strike could pot black for one point, then pot the same ball again for another seven points. Similarly, if only the colours were left, he could pot any of the remaining five colours and claim the two-point value of the yellow.

IN-OFF The cue ball goes into a pocket by mistake, usually after it has struck another ball.

JUMP SHOT The cue ball jumps over any ball, whether accidentally or by design except when it first strikes the object ball before jumping another ball.

KICK The cue ball and object ball do not react as usual, causing both to be thrown off-course. Various theories have been put forward to explain the phenomenon, including static, heat or room temperature, or even surplus chalk left on a ball.

MAXIMUM 147-break, compiled by taking 15 reds, 15 blacks and all six colours in sequence.

MISCUE The cue ball is struck incorrectly, probably through lack of chalk on the tip, causing it to rise momentarily.

NAP The pile on the green cloth like velvet which is ironed in the same direction, up the table from the baulk end. The lower it is trimmed or 'dressed' the faster it plays.

OBJECT BALL Red or colour to be struck by the white.

PACK The 15 reds placed in a triangle form at the start of a frame.

PLANT The object ball (red) is played on to another red to pot it.

POT The object ball is pocketed.

PUSH SHOT The cue ball and the tip of the cue remain in contact as the ball moves forward, or the tip stays in contact with the white when it makes contact with the object ball.

REST An implement on which to balance the cue for out-of-reach shots. There are various types, including full-butt (about 9 ft, cue and rest), half-butt (7 ft) and spider.

SAFETY SHOT When the cue ball is placed to make things awkward for the opponent, leaving him little chance of scoring. This shot has gained in importance in recent years as snooker has become more competitive and the standard of play has improved.

SCREW Making the cue ball travel backwards by means of spin.

SIDE A means of making the cue ball react in various ways to enhance positional play.

SNOOKER The name of the game and also the ultimate safety shot, where a player is unable to strike an object ball directly because another ball or balls on the table is a hazard.

STRIKER A person in play or about to play.

STUN Stopping the cue ball dead on impact.

INDEX